THE QUEEN MOTHER

Lady Elizabeth Bowes-Lyon aged seven.

OVERLEAF HM The Queen Mother photographed for her seventy-fifth birthday by Norman Parkinson.

TITLE PAGE The Duchess of York.

Elizabeth Longford

THE QUEEN MOTHER

Weidenfeld and Nicolson, London

First published in Great Britain by
Weidenfeld and Nicolson Ltd
91 Clapham High Street
London SW4 7TA

ISBN 297 779 761

Colour separations by Newsele Litho Ltd
Printed in Italy by L.E.G.O., Vicenza
Filmset by Keyspools Ltd, Golborne, Lancs.

The Author's Acknowledgments

I would like to thank all those who have kindly allowed me to consult them, especially Lady Salisbury, Lady Diana Cooper, Lord David Cecil, Sir Martin Gilliat, Lady Jean Rankin, the Hon. Mrs John Mulholland, Lord and Lady Adeane, Major Tom Harvey, Sir Oliver Millar, the Duke of Grafton, Professor Ragnhild Hatton, Lady Donaldson, Mrs Peter Cazalet, Lord Charteris, Sir John Colville, Sir Edward Ford, Lord Gage, Lord Head, Lord Glendevon, Mrs Elizabeth Johnston and Mr Woodrow Wyatt. My thanks are also due to those who have sent information, to Christopher Warwick for captioning the illustrations, and to Felicity Luard, Kate Dunning and Lucy Shankleman of Weidenfeld and Nicolson for their work on the manuscript and photographs.

I am grateful to the following for permission to quote from their publications: William Collins, Sons & Co., (Harold Nicolson's *Diaries*), Michael Russell (Lady Diana Cooper's *Autobiography*), John Murray Publishers (Lyttelton – Hart-Davis *Letters II*), and Weidenfeld & Nicolson (Cecil Beaton's *Diaries*).

Contents

OPPOSITE *Detail from a portrait painted in 1925 by De Lazlo. The Countess of Strathmore asked for it to be under life-size, to emphasize her daughter's small, graceful build.*

RIGHT *HM Queen Elizabeth The Queen Mother photographed by Cecil Beaton in the year of her daughter's Coronation, 1953.*

The Lady Elizabeth

1

IT IS USUALLY rash to make sweeping assertions about human beings. But the subject of Queen Elizabeth the Queen Mother seems to invite a certain boldness. She is without doubt the most popular Queen Consort in our history. If that is unquestionable, the questions begin to crowd in when we wonder how she has done it.

Is it perhaps due to her being the first truly British Queen Consort for hundreds of years? No doubt her predecessor, Queen Mary, was British compared with *her* royal predecessors: Alexandra of Denmark, Adelaide of Saxe-Meiningen, Caroline of Brunswick-Wölfenbuttel, Charlotte of Mecklenburg-Strelitz, Caroline of Brandenburg-Anspach, Sophie Dorothea of Brunswick and Celle ... Yet even Queen Mary had a German father, HH Francis Duke of Teck. Though she was born in Kensington Palace like Queen Victoria, she spent much of her penurious youth abroad, visiting continental relations. Mary of Teck's ramrod stance always had something Germanic, if endearing, about it.

To find a drop of non-British blood in the Queen Mother's veins, one must turn back to the seventeenth century in *Burke's Peerage*, when Hans William Bentinck of the Netherlands made his elegant appearance as William III's Groom of the Stole and the Queen Mother's great-great-great-great-great-grandfather, through her mother, Cecilia Cavendish-Bentinck.

On the paternal side, as we shall see, she is descended from subjects, albeit peers of the realm. Add 'commoner', therefore, to 'British', and you have something most unusual in the make-up of a modern Queen Consort. These two facts, however, go but a short way to explain the glow of warmth in which this Queen is held. Today people find it almost impossible to mention her name without calling down a special blessing upon her. In her 1968 diary, for instance, Barbara Castle described a reception for the Cabinet at the Palace, when Her Majesty the Queen Mother looked as 'bouffant as ever – bless her'. The universal affection in which she is held, indeed, can only be explained by the full story of her life.

The future Queen Consort was born on 4 August 1900 in England, of an English mother. That surely makes her half English. Nevertheless it was to Scotland that the baby girl travelled for her first holiday; her father was Scottish. So it is in Scotland that her beginnings must be traced.

Elizabeth Angela Marguerite Bowes-Lyon was the ninth child (she had

OPPOSITE *The eight-year-old Lady Elizabeth Bowes-Lyon. Watercolour by Mabel Hankey.*

five elder brothers and three sisters, one of whom died in childhood) of the 14th Earl of Strathmore and Kinghorne, Lord Glamis. For the last two hundred years or so, her ancestors had been outstanding Scottish landowners, impregnable in their Forfarshire castle of Glamis, with its turreted silhouette like a French château, and walls as solid as the distant Grampian hills. But go back a few centuries further, and you find eruptions of violence that in no way belie the family's armorial bearing of two lions rampant and six cross-bows – the lions of course being for Lyon and the bows for Bowes.

A Lord Glamis was slain at the battle of Sherriffmuir in 1715; another died in a scuffle with Lord Crawford's men in 1578; a Lady Glamis, widowed and remarried, was burned as a witch in 1537; a Lord Glamis and two brothers fell at the battle of Flodden in 1513; another Lyon was killed by another Crawford in 1382. And those were only some especially memorable incidents. The family fortunes, as opposed to misfortunes, dated from the marriage of Jean, daughter of King Robert II, to Sir John Lyon in 1367. This ancestor, known as 'The White Lyon' because of his fair hair, was given Glamis Castle with his bride. He handed down the castle to his family and perhaps also the fair hair; for Elizabeth's youngest brother David was as blond as she was black haired.

King George VI and Queen Elizabeth, incidentally, were to have a common ancestor in Robert Bruce.

As a baby, Elizabeth Bowes-Lyon was forward and venturesome. She crawled, walked and talked early, remembered her nurse Clara Knight ('Alah'). As a child she was already saturated in the history of her Scottish home. This was partly through her own vivid response to the past. She loved dragging period costumes from the family acting-chest and sweeping through Duncan's Hall at Glamis in the crimson velvet and lace collars of the seventeenth century. She liked best of all to be a princess. 'I am Princess Elizabeth,' she would say, the future Winter Queen of Bohemia, daughter of James VI of Scotland and I of England. The lines of this romantic robe that she dressed up in as a seven-year-old were to reappear at her wedding and to be faintly discernible at her Coronation.

But knowledge of history was also a family 'must'. Professional guides to stately homes did not then exist, for family houses were not generally open to the public. So when Lady Strathmore had visitors it would as likely as not be the daughter at home, Elizabeth, who would do the artistic and historic honours. She is remembered as a young Castle guide whose enthusiasm was controlled by common sense. Ghosts? Yes, there were Old Beardie, the White Lady, the Grey Lady and Jack the Runner – enough ghosts to furnish any self-respecting Scottish castle. But Elizabeth sounded a little sceptical. 'That's the ghost,' she would say when they passed a tick-tocking grandfather clock. And later, 'Have you heard about the ghosts?' she asked her friend Betty Cavendish who had come to stay, implying that she didn't believe in them.

As to the 'Monster of Glamis', the castle was so ancient that a deformed heir – this was the legend – could easily have been kept alive for

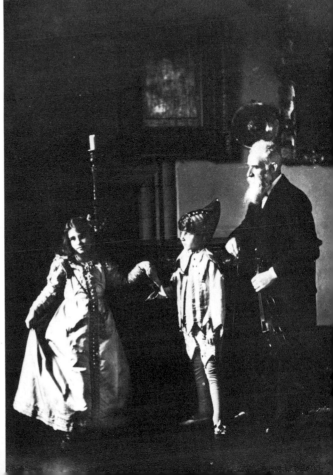

Glamis Castle, ancestral home of the Strathmores.

years in the thickness of its walls. Most family trees, if closely examined, would reveal some spoilt fruits that have fallen off the branches and become conveniently forgotten; the medieval appearance of Glamis lent itself to a legend of 'monstrous' proportions.

Besides ghostly visitants, the young Elizabeth would have to tell of more historic guests: Bonnie Prince Charlie slept there, and so did Sir Walter Scott. Scott found his turret chamber creepy: the living seemed too far away and the dead too near. Others, however, were to find that the sights and sounds of Glamis gave them 'an agreeable creep', especially the sound of bagpipes dying away in the distance, as the pipers marched out of the dining-room after circling the table three times.

It was said that the most unlucky visitors to Glamis were King Malcolm II and his grandson King Duncan I, both murdered there. Macbeth was held to have slain Duncan in the banqueting hall (though neighbouring Cawdor Castle put in the same claim). Shakespeare, as Glamis' most famous visitor, is said to have conceived his play *Macbeth* there. Duncan in fact was murdered at Pitgaveny near Elgin, though Malcolm II certainly died at Glamis. He was 'laid to die' in 'the anteroom by the drawing room', wrote a relation, Constance Smith, in her journal, 'where the door was taken away because it would *not* remain shut'. (Constance was *née* Adeane and a Stanley of Alderley on her maternal side, grandmother of the present Duke of Grafton and a great friend of Elizabeth's mother, Cecilia, Lady Strathmore.)

'The Bentinck blood', she wrote to her daughter from Glamis on 27 August 1908, '... is doing its work in the Lyon family. Cecilia is a piece of absolute perfection and I love Lord Strathmore.' One morning he was bemoaning the 'desperate amount of duties' attached to his lot as a great landowner. '"The Duke of Leeds is a wise man." "Why?" said I. "Why? – well, he yachts a good deal – & he shoots – & then he hunts – & enjoys himself" – "WISE" – says Cecilia firmly from the sidetable – "do you call *that* wise?"'

One may guess that Queen Elizabeth the Queen Mother has occasionally had to use that firm Bentinck voice.

Constance Smith (then Adeane) had seen Glamis in 1861, and recalled the 'vast gloomy mass of building, with a still gloomier interior'. A friend of hers who had visited it nine years earlier remembered the 'alarming Bears that were kept with a pole in the courtyard'. But when Constance Smith returned to stay at Glamis in 1908, Lady Strathmore had transformed the living rooms, some with rich Italian furniture and brocades.

I remember the bright breakfast table [wrote Constance] – Cecilia had a vase of the light heavenly blue Ipomea by her plate to enjoy the colour; the sons chaffed her, Lord Strathmore gently lamented over things, David and Elizabeth ran in and out.

These two youngest children stuck in Constance's mind:

... the two little ones, David and Elizabeth – sweet creatures, Elizabeth lovely. David was an imp – who wanted to be revenged on me for something I had innocently repeated to his mother, and stole my long telephone and ran away with it all over the Castle to Cecilia's despair ... Before leaving Glamis I must note the morning service in the Chapel and the lovely group of Cecilia sitting between David and Elizabeth, Cecilia and Elizabeth wearing little caps, for it is the custom of Glamis not to let a woman creature attend the service with her head uncovered.

A photograph of the Chapel, adds Constance, showed a ghost-lady kneeling there when the plate was developed.

When Elizabeth was not being a Castle guide or assistant hostess to her mother, she was going below stairs to ask for 'more – lots more of that lovely cake; I didn't like to eat it all while it was upstairs.' For she dearly loved what J. M. Barrie in nearby Kirriemuir described in *Peter Pan* as 'rich ... damp ... cake ...' She was known to be critical not to say naughty. The arrival of a new governess provoked the entry in her diary, 'Some governesses are nice, some are *not*.' She once shredded her new sheets with a pair of scissors. Her mother said, 'Oh, Elizabeth.' That was all; but said in such a reproachful voice that Elizabeth immediately repented.

If Scotland was the most powerful influence on her imagination, there was also a tranquil southern home for Elizabeth Bowes-Lyon to grow up in – St Paul's Walden Bury, in Hertfordshire, which had come to the Strathmores from their Bowes ancestors. The name 'St Paul's' came from its having originally been the property of the Chapter of St Paul's Cathedral; while the word 'Walden' meant woods – deep woods lay on one side of the house, divided up by alleys with a small temple once at the end of each.

OPPOSITE *St Paul's Walden Bury*.

The woods were haunted [wrote Constance in her 1908 journal] and now and then processions might be seen going along the alleys. Strange noises were also heard in one or two rooms in the house, but I do not think anything was seen.

The charming Queen Anne mansion was built of red brick and in summer wreathed itself in honeysuckle and magnolia. While there was hardly a garden to speak of at Glamis until Lady Strathmore made one, St Paul's Walden Bury had an elegantly laid out garden with copses and flowers, besides the alleys, for which Le Nôtre, the famous French landscape artist, has been given credit. Most credit, however, for the vision of this garden and home must go to the retentive memory of Lady Elizabeth herself, who jotted down a list of its delights for a friend, after her marriage.

'At the bottom of the garden,' she wrote in the third person, 'is The Wood – the haunt of fairies, with its anemones and ponds and moss-grown statues, and the big oak under which she reads and where the two ring-doves contentedly coo in their wicker-work "Ideal Home". There are carpets of primroses to sit on and her small brother David is always with her ...'

Her memories were later amplified for *The Times* before her Coronation, when she remembered especially the retreats and secret hiding-places – 'a friendly still-room, the attic of a tumbledown brewhouse to play truant in' – and the demanding crowd of little animals that were as much part of the family as her own brothers and sisters.

The Bowes-Lyon children always called themselves 'a clan' rather than a family, so large and yet close-knit were they; and together with the chickens, bantams, bullfinches, doves, dogs, tortoises, Persian kittens, 'Bobs' the Shetland pony and two pet pigs, they resembled one of the tribes in those Bible stories that their mother read aloud until they knew them by heart. The two pigs had comically ill-assorted names, Satan and Emma, like the rocking-horses of Princess Elizabeth and Princess Margaret, one named Caesar and the other Bluebell.

Some of the 'moss-grown statues' also had nicknames: the Frying-pan for a stone basin, the Running Footman for a Greek god and the Bounding Butler for the discus thrower.

Those were the days when the grand aristocracy moved almost like royalty about the country from home to home, three or four times a year. 'The Strathmores were so grand that you didn't notice they were grand at all.' They were piloted by an army of servants. Butlers were kings below stairs and prime ministers upstairs. One family called their butler 'The Mentor'. And little girls fell in love with footmen. 'That's James, I'm going to marry him when I get older,' said Elizabeth one day, James being a footman and the demon bowler of the home team.

For the social season, the family would be installed in 20 St James's Square, London, where Elizabeth and David could look out from their high windows upon the statue of William III, patron of their Bentinck ancestor.

Besides St Paul's Walden Bury, there was another Bowes home which

BELOW LEFT *Lady Elizabeth and her brother David strike an Edwardian pose*.

BELOW RIGHT *Side-saddle at St Paul's Walden Bury*.

Lady Elizabeth, photographed by E.O. Hoppe, during the first year of the Great War.

the Strathmores visited for a few weeks each year – Streatlam Castle in County Durham – for the wealth of the Bowes family was solidly based in the industrial North. Such wealth was not unattractive to the Scottish nobility, and in 1767 the 9th Earl of Strathmore married a young heiress, Mary Eleanor Bowes, 'a little woman, a longish Face, with fine dark brown Hair'. Her father, an MP, racehorse breeder and scholar, founded the fabulous Bowes Museum which still dominates the wild Durham moorland. He brought up his gifted only child to possess considerable book-learning but only 'comparative' religion. As a result she became a distinguished botanist but an unhappy wife. Her misfortunes culminated in her seduction by a cold-hearted rogue who forced her by guile to marry him after she was widowed, took her name of Bowes (his own name was Stoney, a more appropriate one), dissipated her fortune and destroyed her botanical specimens. It is possible, however, to think of poor Mary Eleanor's botanical skill surviving in the love of plants and gardens shown by her descendants, Sir David Bowes-Lyon and his sister the Queen Mother.

It was a sad and solemn moment when David, that younger brother who was 'always with her', went away to school. Their mother had called them her 'two Benjamins', the delightfully unexpected tail-end of her ten children. Now her youngest daughter remained behind, to make the most of what was offered in the way of education to the daughters of the nobility before the First World War.

A school career was rare indeed. Even in families of an age-group somewhat younger than the Strathmores, the older girls still found their instruction in the schoolroom with governesses. True, Lady Strathmore did try out some less conventional ideas on her 'Benjamina'. For she was herself the daughter of a clergyman, and the clergy were often enthusiasts for girls' education. For a short while Elizabeth had enjoyed a nursery-class in London, later to be followed by two terms at a girls' day school, where she won an essay prize. But there were several reasons why the latter experiment did not seem justified.

First, Lady Strathmore, a woman of distinguished mind and character, believed in culture and the arts for girls rather than academic studies. She herself taught all her children to read, and gave her two youngest their first music, dancing and drawing lessons. Second, the atmosphere of school was strange for a thirteen-year-old, used to the company of grown-ups. At St James's Square, in particular, she would meet her parents' friends, like Lord Rosebery, much as the young Princess Victoria had met politicians as a child and learned to talk naturally with the formidable Lord Palmerston. Third, a charming German governess came to look after Elizabeth and David in the Easter holidays of 1913; and Kathie Kuebler was persuaded to stay on. Fräulein Kuebler has left one of the most visual memories of a child who had been such 'an easy and happy baby'. At thirteen, she had 'a small delicate figure, a sensitive, somewhat pale little face, dark hair and very beautiful violet-blue eyes.' The governess found her charge 'far more mature and understanding than her years warranted.'

This 'prematurity' was always to be the fate of Elizabeth Bowes-Lyon, whether as child, wife, or widow. When she was still quite young the cry would go up, 'Where's Elizabeth?' It meant that some visitor felt neglected. 'Easy' herself since babyhood, the child could be relied on to make other people feel at ease. 'Shall us talk now?' she once asked an elderly guest, after pouring tea for him in the temporary absence of her mother. As a young wife, she would be pitched headlong into the royal maelstrom; in itself an experience calculated to make a girl 'far more mature and understanding than her years warranted'. Her widowhood also ran true to form, for it occurred well before the normal time; at fifty-two she would be given the cruel experience that most women do not face until their sixties or seventies. And yet, as we shall see, an eternal youthfulness has developed alongside those very years which at each stage brought too early a maturity. And if the slight fairy-like figure was to vanish with the years, Elizabeth was to achieve something much more remarkable: the majesty and stateliness of a queen, despite her small stature. Hers would be the beauty of an Elizabethan ship in full sail, ready to meet any towering Armada that might come her way.

Up to the age of fourteen, little Elizabeth's experience of social life matched the freedom and gaiety of her own spirit. She enjoyed the usual festivities, and caused small boys to fall in love with her at first sight and remain bewitched until a new stage in their education intervened. Lord David Cecil met her at a dancing class in Lansdowne House, he six and she seven. Playing with her and the yellow-haired David Bowes-Lyon in Hyde Park became a daily treat to be looked forward to for two blissful years. He remembers 'great sweetness and sense of fun; and a certain roguish quality. The personality which I see now was there already.' Since then the threads of that childish romance have been woven, like so many of Queen Elizabeth's early relationships, into a strong friendship – always very naturally expressed and never allowed to lapse.

Suddenly childhood was over. The scene was London on 4 August 1914. She went to the theatre that night. Wild excitement; not because it was her fourteenth birthday, but because war was breaking out and an epoch ending.

The Bowes-Lyon family met the war literally four-square: four brothers at once enlisting, one soon to be killed and another taken prisoner, severely wounded. Meanwhile, batches of wounded soldiers were sent to the hospital that Glamis Castle had now become, and where Lady Strathmore and her daughter Elizabeth acted as hostesses. (An elder sister, Lady Rose, was training as a nurse.) In later years Lady Elizabeth would remember her 'war' as a fury of 'knitting, knitting, knitting', varied by crumpling tissue paper to stuff sleeping-bags. But the many tales told by soldiers who returned home showed that she had found time to hearten the occupants of the long ward set up in the dining-room. To one she was 'a corker', and her kindly approach 'great medicine'. To another she had 'a very taking way of knitting her forehead when speaking'. To yet others she was a partner at whist, an entertainer with popular songs and home-made theatricals, or just a tomboy who let off steam by riding her bicycle 'without hands' and dressed up her brother David as a female visitor. When she required cash from her father she demanded it with panache: 'S.O.S., L.S.D., R.S.V.P.' The young Winston Churchill had once made the same request in much the same code. It was she who almost certainly saved Glamis and its treasures in 1916 when the keep caught fire, by telephoning for *two* fire brigades, the local one and the larger unit from Dundee. A Lyon would never do things by halves.

The war ended at last, the Armistice was signed on 11 November 1918, and Glamis gradually returned to normal. 'Normality' for a girl of Lady Elizabeth's background involved resumption of social life in the South. Her parents gave her a coming-out dance. Elizabeth ran a high temperature on the day; but characteristically she insisted on holding the dance, so as not to disappoint her friends. She enjoyed every moment. Afterwards Lady Buxton, daughter of Constance Smith and one of Lady Strathmore's circle, wrote to a friend: 'Elizabeth Lyon is out now, and Cecilia has had a dance for her. How many hearts Elizabeth will break.'

Not that the 'coming out' of Lord Strathmore's youngest daughter bore any resemblance to the feverish rejoicing of post-war London. Old Lady Airlie, shrewd lady-in-waiting to Queen Mary, had observed her young friend from her own home in neighbouring Cortachy Castle. 'Lady Elizabeth,' she wrote, 'was very unlike the cocktail-drinking, chain-smoking girls who came to be regarded as typical of the 1920s.'

The Ladies Elizabeth and Rose Bowes-Lyon at Glamis, receiving a convalescent soldier.

Lord David Cecil describes her as 'a noticeable debutante' partly because she dressed 'picturesquely, unfashionably'. Indeed, the Strathmore life-style in London was in some respects old-fashioned. An elderly family coachman and no less ancient horse would bring Lady Elizabeth home from her dances. One night the brougham gradually came to a halt in the middle of the road. The surprised debutante put her head out of the window and asked what had happened. 'It's the horse, my lady; he's just having a little sleep.'

But if her horse was tired, Lady Elizabeth's own vitality was 'radiant', to use Lady Airlie's word. To this vitality was added 'gaiety, kindness and sincerity' – a combination that 'made her irresistible to men'.

Some of the Queen Mother's biographers have questioned the statement in Sir John Wheeler-Bennett's *Life of King George VI* that she 'took London by storm'. They doubt whether a girl whose keynote was naturalness and sincerity could have 'stormed' the London of bobbed hair, short skirts and the long weekend. But her old friends agree that this was indeed so. All the men were at her feet. One devoted admirer still remembers the magical atmosphere she created.

I was madly in love with her. Everything at Glamis was beautiful, perfect. Being there was like living in a Van Dyck picture. Time, and the gossiping, junketing world, stood still. Nothing happened. Nothing, except that the seventeen-stone Leveson-Gower [married to her sister Rose] was once thrown out of bed by a ghost. But the magic gripped us all. I fell *madly* in love. They all did.

She had a charm which this life-long admirer could only describe, when pressed, as 'indescribable' – an 'indefinable atmosphere'. She was also very kind and compassionate. 'And she could be very funny – which was rare in those circles. She was a wag.'

Another besotted young man tried to advance his suit with surprising roughness. After a night-long hunt ball, he made the remaining hours of sleep hideous by cracking his hunting-whip under her window.

There was yet another young man whose courtship began quietly and slowly, the way she would have approved. Elizabeth met Prince 'Bertie' at a children's party and gave the shy ten-year-old the cherries off the top of her cake. She was five. Eight years later she may have partnered him at a junior dance, she still in the 'governess' stage, he a naval cadet at Osborne. This was 1913. Three years afterwards she had appeared briefly in London wearing a demure pink bonnet, as a bridesmaid to her sister Rose. *He* had appeared equally briefly in a gun-turret of HMS Collingwood, during the Battle of Jutland. After that exciting summit, ill health forced him out of the Navy, into a branch of the future Royal Air Force, to a Civil Service desk, up to Cambridge, into industrial welfare and social service.

Meanwhile the season of 1920 came round. He met Lady Elizabeth Bowes-Lyon again at a dance given by Lord and Lady Farquhar on 20 May. He is said to have seized her metaphorically from his equerry's arms, with the words, 'That's a lovely girl you've been dancing with. Who is she?' If this legend can scarcely be accurate (for Lady Elizabeth was already a close friend of his sister Princess Mary), there is no doubt he did suddenly recognize 20 May as a red letter day in his life. Like the rest of them, he was madly in love with the Lady Elizabeth.

There were other pleasures that summer. In June his father King George V created him Duke of York. In July he and Commander Louis Greig won the Royal Air Force tennis doubles at Wimbledon. But it was visits to Glamis and St Paul's Walden Bury that really lit up the next months for the new royal Duke. A friend of her many brothers, he began to bask in their youngest sister's 'radiant vitality'. We have seen something of the sturdy ancestry, romantic homes and bubbling family life that had gone to make up her mixture of calm confidence and zest. By way of contrast, a cross fairy seemed to have looked in upon his christening, bringing him more than his fair share of ill luck.

Whereas the baby Elizabeth had been an entirely welcome after-thought, considerably younger than the brother immediately above her, Prince Albert picked the worst possible date for his birthday – 14 December 1895, exactly thirty-four years after the Prince Consort's death, as his great-grandmother Queen Victoria was shocked to realize. And he was the second son born to parents who wanted a girl. Much ingenuity has been spent on analysing the serious effect on this second child of having an elder brother who seemed totally to outshine him; but much less on the effects of having Princess Mary, the family's only girl, so close on his heels.

The elder brother David had more charm than Bertie, robuster health, and a spontaneity that amounted to brilliance. Into the bargain he had straight legs and was Prince of Wales; while Bertie suffered gastric troubles from infancy and was kept in splints for a time to straighten his legs. Nor was it his legs only that were in splints. He was left-handed, and, being forced by his father to use his right hand, he found his tongue also held in bonds, as it were, by a frustrating stammer. Fear of his father's impatient outbursts probably also caused him to catch his breath – no help to a stammerer.

At the same time, golden-haired Princess Mary was her father's favourite. She was high-spirited, a relatively uninhibited spark in a loving but otherwise constrained family. Strange that this Princess, whose very existence in childhood could do nothing but exacerbate Prince Albert's problem, should later be instrumental in achieving his happiness.

For that was how it happened. Lady Elizabeth first knew Princess Mary through the Girl Guides. Then Lady Airlie took a hand. She invited Princess Mary to stay at Cortachy and Prince Bertie came over to Glamis

Rarely seen in uniform, England's future Queen receives a gift from the Girl Guides, 1923.

from Balmoral. They all met. There were charades and sing-songs around the piano. The Prince was enchanted. He had never experienced such relaxed, amusing family life before.

The nearest thing he knew was perhaps his own 'Duke of York's Camp', where he was making the experiment of bringing together boys from public school and working-class homes. Sing-songs were quite a feature of the family life he built up in his annual camp. And incidentally, the originality of his experiment should not be missed. In those days, the idea of boys who were socially poles apart holidaying together was virtually unheard of.

The Duke had been moved to action by the embittered temper of post-war Britain. Ex-servicemen swelled the ranks of the unemployed, instead of occupying the 'Homes fit for Heroes' promised them by the Prime Minister, Lloyd George. Things were to get worse in the next decade. But whereas David, when he became King Edward VIII, would be ready with eloquent words – 'Something must be done, something *will* be done' he told the Welsh miners – his less fluent brother *did* something.

After the first visit to Glamis in autumn 1920, Prince Bertie knew that his heart was set on one girl alone. The hints he dropped to Queen Mary made her aware of the situation in regard to Lady Elizabeth. 'She seems a charming girl,' the Queen confided to Lady Airlie, 'but I don't know her very well.'

However, there was to be a setback to Prince Bertie's hopes, but the kind of setback that spurred on this determined character to greater efforts.

In the following spring (1921) he told his parents that he was going to propose. King George V immediately, in his tough naval way, conveyed pleasure at his second son's choice, qualified by doubt of his success. 'You will be a lucky fellow if she accepts you.'

But Lady Airlie saw that her young friend Elizabeth would also be 'lucky' if she was moved to love the Duke. Informal chats with each of them separately convinced Lady Airlie of his sterling qualities and also of his touching devotion. 'He was deeply in love but so humble,' she wrote in her memoirs, *Thatched with Gold*. It was Lady Airlie also who realized what would hold the twenty-year-old girl back, if and when the Duke asked her to marry him. 'She was frankly doubtful,' wrote Lady Airlie, 'uncertain of her feelings and afraid of the public life which would lie ahead of her as the King's daughter-in-law.'

No doubt that second reason – fear of royal 'public life' – was the operative one. Even today a twenty-year-old girl might hesitate before dipping her toe into the magical dew-pond of royal life. It would be lovely to dance in a fairy-ring for ever, with no chores, no traffic jams, no queues. Looked at from inside, however, that magic circle might seem more like a noose: unremitting public service of a specially repetitive and conventional kind, from which there was no escape. Yet today the royal circle is nothing like so tight and restricted as it was while King George V and Queen Mary reigned.

Queen Victoria's granddaughter Princess Alice, who died in 1981

'I know I am very lucky,'
Prince Albert wrote to his
mother, Queen Mary,
when Lady Elizabeth
finally said 'yes'. An
engagement study.

aged ninety-seven years, wrote down her views on the subject of royal qualities and royal service. The strain of lifelong service was still immense, she believed, even in 1965. 'None but those trained from youth to such an ordeal can sustain it with amiability and composure.'

The future Queen Elizabeth had not been trained from youth for this ordeal, and at twenty she was wide awake to the fact. Of course with hindsight we can see that her actual training was as good or better than that of a royal princess. All that precocious yet spontaneous and unaffected entertaining of her mother's guests; all that care and concern for the sick and wounded in Glamis . . . It was a quasi-royal training, with the starch taken out of it. Moreover, in the summer of 1921 Lady Strathmore herself fell ill, and Lady Elizabeth had to act as hostess both at shooting-parties and during a further royal visit to Glamis.

So the Duke of York was refused and everyone was sad. Lady Airlie spoke of her own frank disappointment, and Lady Strathmore was sorry to see the Duke's disconsolate face. 'I like him so much,' she said, 'and he is a man who will be made or marred by his wife.' Queen Mary still saw Elizabeth Bowes-Lyon as 'the one girl who could make Bertie happy'.

Though disconsolate at first, the Duke of York sensed that the clouds were not impenetrable. That summer he wrote from Glamis: 'It is delightful here and Elizabeth is very kind to me. The more I see her, the more I like her.' Elizabeth was indeed too genuinely kind to go on encouraging a devotion she could never reciprocate.

Then Princess Mary again took a hand, by inviting Lady Elizabeth to be a bridesmaid at her wedding to Viscount Lascelles on 28 February 1922. Sheathed in silver tissue, the twenty-one-year-old bridesmaid had

Lady Elizabeth flanked by her father, Lord Strathmore, and her eldest brother, Lord Glamis, just before her marriage.

her first glimpse of what it was to participate in a royal public event. With her flair for happiness, she could not but find it enjoyable.

Throughout 1922 the romantic relationship on both sides developed. The Duke of York, becoming more at ease with this close-knit but welcoming family of Bowes-Lyon, 'blossomed'. (This was the well-chosen expression of his official biographer, who had seen the Duke's private notes and letters in the Royal Archives.) The emotional inhibitions formed by twenty-seven years spent in singularly undemonstrative surroundings began to dissolve. On the other side, Lady Strathmore noticed for the first time that Elizabeth was 'really worried'. The roles of the two young people had in fact been reversed, the Duke becoming the assured one, and the usually calm Lady Elizabeth being uncertain. 'I think she was torn,' added her mother, 'between her longing to make Bertie happy and her reluctance to take on the responsibilities which this marriage must bring.'

On a Saturday morning in January 1923 the now debonair young Prince tried again, this time during a walk through the winter trees at St Paul's Walden Bury. It was the same wood that Elizabeth as a child had realized was 'the haunt of fairies' and where the anemones would reappear in the spring. No doubt her companion now felt that the fairies had reappeared too. He had devised a two-word message with which to notify his parents if she accepted him. That afternoon of the 13th a telegram went off to Sandringham, 'ALL RIGHT' – signed 'BERTIE'. It was the luckiest 13th in both their lives. 'I know I am very lucky,' he wrote to Queen Mary three days later, 'to have won her over at last.'

Duchess of York

2

THREE MONTHS after her engagement, Lady Elizabeth Bowes-Lyon became HRH the Duchess of York. She made her wedding preparations with an eye to the times. No mink or sable (though the King gave her an ermine coat) but squirrel and 'lapin'. When the people of Forfarshire asked what she would like as a wedding present, she preferred an illuminated scroll to a costly gift. The twenty-four varieties of wellingtons and galoshes presented by the Pattenmakers seemed to foreshadow her prowess at fishing.

The chosen wedding-day was 26 April 1923 and the place Westminster Abbey. Lord Strathmore left 17 Bruton Street, the family's new London home, with his daughter at 11.12 a.m. precisely. This was her first taste of rigorous royal punctuality.

The last King's son to be married in the Abbey had been King Richard II, to Anne of Bohemia in 1382. So the small girl who had dressed up as the Winter Queen was now indeed following in the footsteps of a princess of Bohemia.

OPPOSITE *The Duchess of York; a watercolour portrait by Savely Sorine, 1923.*

LEFT *Leaving 17 Bruton Street for Westminster Abbey, 26 April 1923*

Elizabeth was no Winter Duchess. She left her parents' home in April showers, but the sun came out as she entered the Abbey's great west door, and it was shining brightly when she emerged, a royal bride, to drive in state back to Buckingham Palace. The Abbey looked austere with no floral decoration, and the bride had managed to get rid of her bouquet before even stepping into the aisle. With a delightful impulsiveness that was never to be totally repressed, she placed her white York roses and Scottish heather on the tomb of the Unknown Warrior, instead of waiting to lay it on the Cenotaph in Whitehall. She had also left her small handbag behind in the carriage, as her daughter Princess Elizabeth was to do twenty-four years later.

The wedding dress had to be of deep ivory to tone with the old lace she had been lent by Queen Mary. In later years, when Norman Hartnell was privileged to design Queen Elizabeth's dresses, he had little good to say of antique lace, though modern Nottingham lace, 'rippling in cataracts of beauty', could not be overpraised. The Duchess's brilliant complexion was certainly guaranteed to outshine old lace and make it look faded.

They were married by the handsome Archbishop of Canterbury, Cosmo Gordon Lang, known to Lady Buxton for his dignity as 'Popey Lang'. This prelate, who was later to show a lack of tact in an Abdication broadcast, now rightly picked out for special remark the bride's closeness to the people. Her friendly upbringing among the country folk of Scotland, he said, had rendered her 'fitted for your place in the people's life'.

Demonstrative crowds welcomed the happy pair in Parliament Square

Bride and bridegroom in the Throne Room at Buckingham Palace after their wedding. With them are the Earl and Countess of Strathmore and Kinghorne and the King and Queen.

and the press hit upon two affectionate titles for this new addition to the Royal Family. They called her either 'the little Duchess' (she was five feet two inches) or 'the smiling Duchess'; for she smiled and waved with spontaneous happiness, as she drove beside her husband through the silver-garlanded streets.

The Times, however, had felt in duty bound to point out that another royal wedding – the Prince of Wales' – would be even more welcome, since it would give 'a future Queen to England'. *The Times* could not know that 'a future Queen' had just stood at the altar.

The Duchess's smiles were to become the most recognizable among her many graces. In those days a smiling royalty was rare. The Victorian age was still close enough for people to remember the old Queen's dictum: that the expression on a royal face could never be 'too earnest'. There is hardly a wisp of a smile in the Yorks' wedding photographs, whether of bride, bridegroom, parents, best man (the Prince of Wales) or bridesmaids.

Changes were to be made in future royal weddings. Never again would there be a formidable eight-course wedding breakfast, lasting ninety minutes and culminating in the cutting by the bride of a pre-sliced nine-foot cake. Fortunately there was only one speech: a toast by the King in his mellifluous deep voice. 'I ask you to drink the health, long life and happiness of the bride and bridegroom.'

The Duchess refused to be bound too strictly by fashion in her going-

A patriotic post-card commemorating the Royal Wedding, 1923. The service was not broadcast lest people should be listening in public houses or wearing hats.

away outfit. Though she accepted the crepe material, subdued shades of grey and beige, barred shoes of a sandal type, long necklace and low waist-line which were all the rage in the early twenties, she rejected the large stylish hat, with its partially concealing brim. Instead she chose a small, off-the-face model, enlivened by a perky feather on one side.

Perhaps to dwell on this little hat is to trivialize the Duchess's wedding-day. But it was symbolic of her lifelong resolve to maintain her 'place in the people's life'. She would let them see her clearly and would herself look them in the face. Lady Strathmore had long ago impressed on her, 'Never look at your feet.' Queen Mary was so shy that she rarely looked anywhere else. It was for the Duchess of York to bring a new look into the Royal Family.

The Prince of Wales, as best man, escorted his brother and sister-in-law to Waterloo Station, for the start of their honeymoon. With justice, he was later to congratulate the Duchess on having 'brought into the family a lively and refreshing spirit'. But oddly enough, he himself was seldom if ever attracted by girls who might be described as a breath of fresh air. Experienced married women, older than himself, and at their best in the exhausted atmosphere of night clubs, were already his preference.

Part of the honeymoon was spent in Mrs Ronald Greville's magnificent house at Polesden Lacey; for Mrs Greville liked to think she had surpassed Lady Airlie as a matchmaker, having promoted the Mountbattens' engagement as well as the Yorks'. The Duchess caught

After leaving London by train ('rather nice, people came and saw one off'), the Duke and Duchess of York honeymoon at the home of society 'matchmaker', Mrs Ronald Greville, Polesden Lacey, May 1923.

whooping cough at Glamis, where they spent the second part of their honeymoon; not very romantic, as she ruefully admitted.

Their first permanent home was a little too romantic, and not nearly convenient enough for a busy young couple. White Lodge, in the depths of Richmond Park, was lent to them as a grace-and-favour house by the King. The splendid deer park had once been Henry VIII's hunting ground and in 1923 the hunt was on – to find the Lodge not the deer. In the fog and darkness of a winter evening, the Yorks' chauffeur could easily lose his way. The house was too big and expensive to keep up properly, even when they economized on the menus. 'I had better warn you that our cook is not very good,' the Duke told his mother the first time that he and his wife invited the King and Queen to dine; 'but she can do the plain dishes & I know you like that sort.'

Queen Mary had a sentimental feeling about White Lodge. She had lived there as a child and the Prince of Wales had been born there. She saw no reason for the King to add further 'grace' to his 'favour' by installing proper central heating.

Not that Queen Mary's intentions were anything but excellent. She consistently sang the Duchess's praises, declaring her pretty, charming and very well brought up. As for the King, 'everyone falls in love with her,' he wrote – including himself. Even his obsession with punctuality melted before her warmth. One evening she and the Duke arrived a few minutes late for dinner. She apologized to the King. 'No, my dear,' he interrupted, 'we must have sat down a few minutes early.'

Her hold on him was twofold. First, she could speak out to him fearlessly. 'I miss him dreadfully,' she was to write to his doctor, Lord Dawson, after his death. 'Unlike his own children I was never afraid of him ...' Second, she felt genuine sympathy towards him and interest in him as a person, quirks and all. One of her rejected suitors had analysed her sympathy as a function of good manners. 'She had frightfully good manners,' he recalled, 'and gave the impression of being riveted by what you said.' No doubt her patience with the protestations of an ardent young man was largely good manners. But in the case of the old King, she not only conveyed an interest in his personality but felt it. He was so '*dependable*' she added in her letter to Lord Dawson. 'And when he was in the mood, he could be deliciously funny too! Don't you think so?'

Nevertheless both King George and Queen Mary were insensitive about the younger generation. Immediately after the Yorks' marriage, King George wrote an extraordinarily revealing note to his son. 'Dearest Bertie,' he began, '... You are indeed a lucky man to have such a charming & delightful wife as Elizabeth.' But he went on, strangely: 'It must have been with a pang that you left your home after 27 years.'

It did not strike the King that 'home' for Bertie was now wherever Elizabeth might be; and the only 'pang' his son felt was that he could not as yet offer her a better home than White Lodge, inaccessibly situated in Richmond Park.

The King ended more realistically, 'I am quite certain that Elizabeth will be a splendid partner in your work ...'

The work that fell to the lot of the Yorks consisted in the bestowing of royal patronage, and the garnering of further experience. Patronage was in a peculiar position during the early twenties. The King had only one daughter-in-law – Elizabeth – so that feminine patronage tended to focus on her. At the same time there was no Welfare State to stretch its net beneath the unfortunate. Voluntary bodies were overwhelmed by the pressures of poverty, ill-health and homelessness after the war. The monarchy itself seemed to be on trial.

The year 1917 had been disastrous for the monarchical principle in Europe. King George v's Russian cousins, the Tsar Nicholas and Tsarina Alexandra, were destroyed in the Bolshevik revolution. Other European thrones were soon to totter and fall. King George himself only escaped from the secondary effects of Kaiser Bill-baiting by changing his family name from the German Coburg, Wettin, or whatever it might be – nobody quite knew – to the English name of Windsor. By the time the British people had got used to their new Royal House of Windsor, the German cousins, too, had gone down the political drain, and there was a republican President in the Potsdam palace.

In a sense all the surviving monarchies were on trial in the twenties. It was the British monarchy's hard work and sense of duty towards the public that saved it from the holocaust.

It was also King George's duty to render all possible psychological aid to his fellow-monarchs – most of them relatives. With this in mind, he sent the Yorks over to the Balkans for the christening of Crown Prince Peter of Yugoslavia, followed next day by the marriage of Prince Paul of Yugoslavia to Princess Olga of Greece. The Duke of York's chief pleasure was derived from Elizabeth's immense popularity with everyone she met. 'They were all enchanted with Elizabeth,' he wrote. 'She was wonderful with all of them & they were all strangers except Paul & Olga.'

Long afterwards there was a personal postscript to this Balkan family celebration. When the Second World War drove the rest of the Balkan princes off their thrones, Prince Paul eventually settled in South Africa. On one of her visits, Queen Elizabeth the Queen Mother called on him there, sunk in misery. It was due to her kindness and vitality that he was aroused from incipient melancholia.

There is something appropriate in the fact that the Duchess began her lifelong work of royal patronage with a visit to the Contemporary Arts Society. She had more feeling for the arts than any other royal personage since the first Prince Albert. But whereas the poor Prince Consort sometimes found his duties a 'treadmill', the Duchess always undertook each one of hers with the zest of a 'first time ever'. An air pageant, an East End children's outing, an official visit with the Duke to Northern Ireland: they all helped to make her face and personality familiar to the public. 'I am very lucky indeed to have her to help me,' said the ecstatic Duke for the hundredth time, 'as she knows exactly what to do & say to all the people we meet.' But she knew it by instinct, not by regal training.

The Duke's camps and work for industrial relations were still his main

social preoccupations. Here the Yorks had a gift in common. Just as the Duchess would never forget the face of a soldier who had recuperated at Glamis during the First World War, so the Duke would recognize an 'old boy' from one of his camps: 'Hallo, you were in my camp ... in such and such a year. How are you getting on?'

In 1924 the Duke had two ambitions. To spend some time in a real jungle camp and to learn something about the Empire, of whose Wembley Exhibition he was to be President the next year. When agreement was wrung from King George, the Yorks spent an eye-opening four months in East Africa, leaving home on 1 December 1924.

After working hard to understand the colonial system of Kenya, the couple revelled in six weeks' safari. They camped out in heat and torrential rains, the Duchess looking attractively workmanlike in a bush shirt, hat and slacks. She shot a rhinoceros among other large animals with her .275 Rigby rifle. The time had not yet come when the Royal Family would lead a wildlife conservation drive and 'shoot' their rhinos with a camera rather than a gun. On this early tour, however, one of the Duke's rhinos got him into a different kind of trouble. The Sabbatarians and their friends denounced him for recklessly allowing himself to be charged by a rhino, and that *on a Sunday*. To which the Duke retorted that he had not been charged by a rhino, and even if he had, he doubted if the rhino would have known it was a Sunday.

The couple returned through Uganda and the Sudan – only to find that an Empire tour, however strenuous, was much more rewarding than an Empire Exhibition, which the nervous Duke had to open before a packed audience, including his formidable Papa. King George conceded that

April 1925 and the Duke and Duchess of York visit the Makwar Dam.

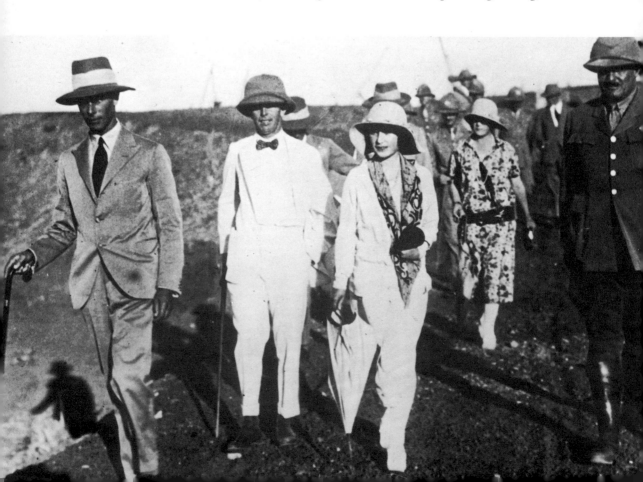

'Bertie got through his speech all right,' despite some 'rather long pauses'. Others were to remember the pauses as 'agonizing'.

To make up for this traumatic event – perhaps the worst speech-making experience of the Duke's life – the Duchess was able to hold out a thrilling prospect for next year. She was expecting her first baby.

Since Queen Mary had given birth to her first-born at White Lodge, she and King George saw no reason why the isolated Lodge should not be the birthplace of their grandchild. The Duchess's mother, however, offered 17 Bruton Street, in the heart of Mayfair. The baby Princess of York was born there at 3.40 a.m. on 21 April 1926. One can imagine the young father's state of nerves, highly strung as he was in any case, for the birth was difficult and the baby delivered by Caesarean section. At least the Duchess had the added pleasure of presenting him with a child of pristine beauty – fair, pink and perfect. 'We always wanted a child to make our happiness complete,' wrote the Duke to his mother.

The Duchess had always wanted a girl. Now she had one, with the same initials as herself: E.A.M., for Elizabeth Alexandra Mary.

The Duke found the new arrival so 'wonderful and strange' that he could hardly believe it. Again through his Duchess, he was to receive another wonderful gift during the year of 1926. The gift of uninhibited speech.

Soon after the baby's birth, King George v decided the Yorks should visit New Zealand and Australia, to open the new Parliament building in Canberra. It was disappointing that they should be uprooted just when their happiness was complete. The Duke had earlier begged his father to send them on an Empire tour, but the King had told the newly-marrieds to 'settle down' first. Now that they were settled down they must be torn up. Not only that, but the stammer which had been so bad on that public day of the Wembley Empire Exhibition would surely be ten times worse during six whole months of publicity in the Empire itself. Here the Duchess intervened. She persuaded her husband to try just once more to get his stammer cured.

Appropriately enough it was an Australian, Lionel Logue, who cured the royal visitor to Australia. With the help of prolonged breathing exercises patiently performed, which the Duchess also studied in order to encourage her husband, the stammer was reduced by autumn 1926 to nothing more than occasional hesitations. The couple's resultant happiness was sensed by Duff Cooper, the future Cabinet Minister and writer, who happened to see them at the theatre just before Christmas. 'The Duke and Duchess of York were there,' he wrote to his wife Lady Diana. 'They are such a sweet little couple [the Duke was taller than Duff!] and so fond of one another. They reminded me of us, sitting together in the box having private jokes, and in the interval ... they slipped out, and I found them standing together in a dark corner of the passage talking happily as we might. She affects no shadow of airs or graces.'

The royal couple set sail in *Renown* on 6 January 1927. For the Duchess there was an almost unbearable moment of parting: 'The baby

OPPOSITE ABOVE *The Duchess with her 'catch' at Lake Wanaka, South Island, New Zealand, in 1927.*

OPPOSITE BELOW *Wellington; the Duchess of York inspects a pack of wolf cubs.*

RIGHT *With Princess Elizabeth : 'The baby was so sweet playing with the buttons on Bertie's uniform that it quite broke me up,' wrote the Duchess on her departure for the Empire.*

BELOW *A Charity fête at Balmoral patronized by the Royal Family. The relaxed mutual affection between King George and his daughter-in-law is very apparent. In the foreground baby Elizabeth is pushed in her pram by her nurse 'Alla'.*

was so sweet playing with the buttons on Bertie's uniform that it quite broke me up.' The voice of duty was a stern one. It called upon her to miss six irreplaceable months of her baby's development. The Strathmore family had never relegated their children to the nursery, as so many parents did in the late nineteenth and early twentieth centuries. For those who did, a parting of six months would not have been greatly noticed. But the Duchess always saw her children on every possible occasion throughout the day, so that to be parted was real suffering.

Both the Duke and Duchess had seminal experiences on their Empire tour. When the Duchess went down with severe tonsillitis in New Zealand, the Duke humbly believed no one would come out on the streets to see him alone. He found he was wrong. And the Duchess's hypnotic effect on a crowd was for the first time remarked upon, when a Communist averred that HRH had looked him straight in the eyes, smiled – and converted him. This gift of seeming to smile at *each one* of several thousand people was to become famous.

Her wit and calm were at a premium on the way home. A fire that broke out in *Renown*'s boiler-room, when they were far from land, was brought under control only just before the flames reached the oil tanks. 'Ma'am, did you realize how bad it was?' asked the Captain afterwards. 'Yes, indeed,' replied the Duchess. 'Every hour someone said there was nothing to worry about, so I knew there was real trouble.'

They returned home in June from this first baptism of unremitting work. Three years before, King George had said of his daughter-in-law, 'everyone falls in love with her.' The rapturous response of the people of Australia and New Zealand now proved this to be true.

Two things had caused the baby Princess Elizabeth's birth to pass off relatively quietly. One was the General Strike of 1926. It almost coincided with her birthday. Lady Diana Cooper has described vividly the transports of fear, energy and hope into which she and her friends were thrown. 'I could hear the tumbrils rolling,' she wrote, 'and heads sneezing into the baskets, and yet and yet, the English could not be like that. Then where would it end?'

The second reason was her position in the Royal Family. True, HRH The Princess Elizabeth of York was now the third in succession to the Throne; her uncle David being first and her father second. Nevertheless, it did not seem very likely that she would succeed before middle age, if ever. She might well have a brother of her own who would take precedence. And even if her uncle the Prince of Wales never married, or married and had no children, he was likely to live for at least the allotted span of three score years and ten. Which indeed he did, though not as reigning monarch. All these considerations carried weight, and incidentally helped the Duchess to bring up her first child in a mild light of publicity rather than a glare.

All the same, there was enormous interest in the little Princess. The people of Australia and New Zealand sent the Duchess back with two tons of toys for her daughter, most of which were sorted out by the Duchess and presented to children's hospitals and homes. Some of the

The Yorks' second daughter was born at Glamis on 21 August 1930. 'Bertie and I have decided to call our little daughter Margaret Rose' wrote the Duchess to Queen Mary.

presents were addressed to 'Princess Betty'. But the Princess's name was never shortened by the family to anything but her own childish invention of 'Lilibet'. King George V adopted this diminutive with enthusiasm, always referring to 'sweet little Lilibet'.

On 21 August 1930, at Glamis, the succession was doubly secured by the birth of a second daughter to the Yorks. The Duchess knew exactly how to handle the King when he made difficulties over the baby's name. The Yorks were set on Ann since 'Ann of York sounds pretty,' wrote the Duchess, '& Elizabeth and Ann go so well together.' For some reason the King vetoed it. Very well, of course the Duchess would accept his decision. But having chosen Margaret Rose instead, she did not put these names to her father-in-law as a suggestion, but to her mother-in-law as a *fait accompli*. 'Bertie & I have decided now to call our little daughter "Margaret Rose" . . . I hope you like it.' There was a firm, though not an iron hand, inside the small velvet glove.

For the next six years the Yorks were to enjoy a state as near to paradise as the human condition allows. Nor was a growing round of royal duties excluded from the Duchess's idea of paradise. She felt a real love for the hospitals and societies she patronized, such as Moorfields Eye Hospital and St Mary's, Paddington, which she was to pray for nightly during the blitz and apparently to save from bombing! In 1927 she had become Colonel-in-Chief of the King's Own Yorkshire Light Infantry, her first regiment, and in the same year a Burgess of the City of Glasgow. In 1928 St John's Ambulance Brigade invited her to be their Commandant-in-Chief. Societies primarily concerned with the welfare of mothers and children naturally clamoured for her patronage; for instance, Dr Barnardo's Middlesex Home. Apart from these permanent interests and many others like them, the smiling Duchess was a favourite for one-day ceremonies, like the official opening of their new building for the Royal College of Obstetrics and Gynaecology in 1932.

Then there were the numerous occasions when she accompanied her

husband on his official duties, using her famous smile to encourage and approve his own increasing mastery of the art of public speaking. 1929 saw them both in Edinburgh, it being the 600th anniversary of the City's charter. The Duke was High Commissioner to the General Assembly of the Church of Scotland (reunited that year) and the Duchess gave a garden party for children at Holyroodhouse. 'The only thing I regret,' she told Queen Mary, 'is that we have not got Lilibet here. Not that they would have seen her, but they would have liked to feel she was here.' So, no doubt would the Duchess.

With that her thoughts returned to the old fear of the royal responsibility that she had taken on, first for herself and now for her daughter. 'It almost frightens me that the people should love her so much,' she continued. 'I suppose that it is a good thing and I hope that she will be worthy of it, poor little darling.'

Lastly there was a cheerful round of social events, such as family weddings, Ascot and other races, and meets when the Duchess would drive up to see her husband set off hunting, though she did not hunt herself. Perhaps all these events were not quite as cheerful as they had been. The slump or depression of the 1930s began with the Wall Street crash of 1929 in America and culminated in Hitler's *coup* in Germany. It brought hardship to two million unemployed and deep anxiety to those, like the Yorks, with social consciences. The Duke, in the course of resorting to more simple living, sold all his beloved hunters.

If for the country the early 1930s were running down a slippery slope towards disaster, the same years in the Yorks' domestic life were exceptionally stable. To begin with, the birth of Lilibet had at last convinced the King that they must have a home of their own. They moved into a stately and comfortable mansion, 145 Piccadilly,

Royal Lodge, Windsor Great Park; the pink-washed house that the Queen Mother was to describe as 'strawberries and cream'. It was camouflaged, to look like 'mud' during the war.

immediately on returning from their world tour. The site seemed almost as soaked in history as White Lodge, and was a great deal more accessible. The two little Princesses could run their races up to Byron's statue and catch sight of the gigantic monument to Wellington not far beyond. How the Great Duke would have idolized the Duchess of York. She was precisely his ideal of womanhood: exquisitely pretty, kind-hearted, attentive, amusing. His home, Apsley House, stands near the site of 145 Piccadilly; but whereas St Mary's Hospital was saved, the bombs got her old home during the Second World War.

The Duchess's own room was the heart of the house. Here she worked; and here her husband and children felt free to come and go – usually to come. When Lilibet reached the age of seven, the Duchess wished to send her to school. But the King vetoed the plan. What? Third in succession to the Throne and going to a school with other children? The conventional idea was still to segregate royal princes and princesses by means of tutors and governesses, a first step in the build-up of a mystique based on remoteness. Fortunately the Duchess was able to see her grandchildren educated for participation rather than isolation. And what would George v have thought if he had known that the result of his insistence on a governess was to be – 'Crawfie'. In 'Alla', once her own nurse, the Duchess had chosen brilliantly for her children. Crawfie – Miss Crawford – though an able woman, could not resist some twenty-five years later the chance to describe to the public her royal service. The Duchess's sympathies, extensive though they were, did not extend to the author of *The Little Princesses*.

Pleasant as their London home was, the Yorks' two happiest retreats were Birkhall in Scotland, not too far from Balmoral, and Royal Lodge in Windsor Great Park, both loaned to them by the King.

Years before, King George IV had made the Royal Lodge into a charming *cottage ornée*, where he could temporarily escape his critics, listen to a boatload of royal fiddlers on Virginia Water, or take the small Princess Victoria's breath away with his avuncular greeting, 'Give us your little paw.' Royal Lodge had since been through many vicissitudes. But in 1934 there were again little royal paws, this time ready and eager to get deliciously grubby in helping their parents restore the over-run gardens to beauty. The whole York family put their backs into work with wheelbarrows and pruning saws. So knowledgeable did the Duke become about his favourite rhododendrons and azaleas (soon to cascade across the future Savill Garden) that when his wife went down with bronchitis he described her pale appearance to a friend in the language of rhododendrons: 'I found her looking Microleucrum (small and white).' An equerry was later to say that he had never known a family more blissfully happy in their home life.

Yet every silver lining has its cloud, and the Yorks' gleaming happiness had its personal anxiety. This was the old King's crumbling health and, part of the same cloud, the Prince of Wales' failure to 'settle down'. In 1928 the King fell so seriously ill that the Duke had to send for his brother

Three-year-old Princess Elizabeth engages her grandfather in conversation at Bognor during the King's convalescence. Queen Mary is with them. 1929.

Silver Jubilee 1935. King George and Queen Mary are received at the West door of St Paul's Cathedral. A painting by Frank Salisbury.

urgently from East Africa. Even in his alarm, the Duke was able to make a joke that reads ironically in the light of coming events: 'There is a lovely story going about,' he wrote to the Prince of Wales, '. . . that the reason of your rushing home is that in the event of anything happening to Papa I am going to bag the throne in your absence!!!! Just like the Middle Ages.' It was not the Duke but quite another character who was to be instrumental in depriving the Prince of his future crown.

Since 1934 the Prince of Wales had transferred his affections from both Freda Dudley Ward and an American married woman named Thelma Furness, to the American wife of a naturalized Englishman, Ernest Simpson. Wallis Warfield Simpson records that she first met the Prince in 1930. Born in Baltimore in 1896, Wallis Warfield had divorced her first husband by 1927, a Lieutenant Winfield Spencer in the American Navy. This first husband was still living, not surprisingly, in 1934. Ernest Simpson had also been through the divorce courts once.

Wallis Simpson was presented to the King and Queen at Buckingham Palace that year. Her chic appearance did not relieve the King's anxiety. There were already rumours about her and the Prince. 'After I am dead,' the King said to Baldwin, 'the boy will ruin himself in twelve months.'

Death was not far off. The Duchess of York had been able to bring comfort to the sick King's last days by sending his 'sweet little Lilibet' to stay with him during a period of convalescence at Bognor. In May 1935 he enjoyed another great satisfaction – his Silver Jubilee. Chips Channon, who was watching the Jubilee procession, commented in his diary first on

the Duchess of York's 'two tiny pink children' and herself 'charming and gracious'; then on the Prince of Wales 'smiling his dentist smile'.

The King gradually sank. Every morning he would still have two particular moments of pleasure. One, when he looked through his binoculars from Buckingham Palace at Lilibet waving to him from a window in 145 Piccadilly. Indeed, one of his last wishes, expressed in his usual explosive way, had been: 'I pray to God that my eldest son will never marry and have children, and that nothing will come between Bertie and Lilibet and the Throne.'

The other pleasure was a daily telephone conversation with his favourite sister, Princess Victoria. 'Is that you, you old fool' this uninhibited character once began, and was not at all daunted to hear the operator reply suavely, 'No, your Royal Highness. His Majesty is not yet on the line.' Then one day it was Princess Toria who was not on the line. She died on 3 December 1935. Broken-hearted and desperately ill, but nevertheless at peace, the King himself died on 20 January 1936.

'My children have all been marvellous,' wrote the widowed Queen Mary in her diary. Her sympathetic daughter-in-law had not been present, owing to her usual winter attack of influenza. Elizabeth was one of those who fought to achieve her good health by sheer will power, just as she fought for everything else that she held to be of value. She would need all her strength for the year that lay ahead.

Daily Mirror

No. 10305   Registered at the G.P.O. as a Newspaper   ONE PENNY

LONDON·ED.

THE KING DECIDES: ABDICATION PLANS

DRAMATIC VISIT TO QUEEN MARY

THE KING HAS DECIDED.

His abdication—unless he makes an eleventh hour change in his decision—is regarded by the Cabinet as imminent.

His Majesty's decision will be announced by Mr. Baldwin in the House of Commons this afternoon. Lord Halifax will make a similar statement in the House of Lords.

Last night the Labour and Liberal Opposition leaders were informed by the Government of the latest moves in the crisis, and advised that there is little hope of a happy solution.

YESTERDAY AFTERNOON THE KING SLIPPED SECRETLY OUT OF FORT BELVEDERE—THE FIRST TIME HE HAD LEFT THE FORT FOR SIX DAYS—AND HE DROVE TO WINDSOR GREAT PARK, WHERE, IN ROYAL LODGE, HE HAD TEA WITH HIS MOTHER, QUEEN MARY.

This meeting was of the most moving character and had been arranged with the utmost privacy.

Elaborate precautions were taken to enable King Edward to leave the Fort unobserved.

Over Rough-Track Roads

To avoid being seen, the King left by one of the rough track roads seldom used by cars and was able to make the two-mile journey without being seen.

His car had only to traverse 200 yards of public roadway before it crossed from his estate into the long private drive through Windsor Great Park to the Lodge.

No one working in the grounds was allowed to see the King leave the house. Workmen were told to remain hidden in a garage.

After spending half an hour with his mother the King returned as secretly to the Fort.

Queen Mary was accompanied by the Princess Royal and the Earl of Athlone. Later she dined with the Duke and Duchess of Kent.

In Mr. Baldwin's private room at the House of Commons last night a special Cabinet meeting was called and Ministers were frankly told of all developments.

The King had a further consultation with his brothers, the Duke of York and the Duke of Kent at Fort Belvedere during the day. The Duke of York did not return to London till 9 p.m. He looked pale and worn. In the event of abdication he will automatically succeed to the Crown.

Throughout the day dispatch riders with important messages from London had arrived at the Fort. The King's car drove out at 8.30 and shortly before eleven o'clock the royal shooting brake which has been used for the transportation of luggage left Fort Belvedere, and also a dispatch rider

The Duke of Kent drove to Marlborough House shortly after 8 o'clock and at 10.15 a large car entered the gates with the Duke of York as its only passenger.

M.P.s warned to be at the House to-day; Mrs. Simpson's drive.—Page 3.

KING EDWARD VIII

DIARY OF THE DAY'S EVENTS

Noon.—Mr. Walter Monckton, K.C., Attorney-General to the Duchy of Cornwall, and Sir E. Peacock back at No. 10.
1.15 p.m.—Cabinet meeting ended.
3.33 p.m.—Mr Baldwin made his statement in Commons
4.5 p.m.—Duke of York arrived at Fort Belvedere.
5.0 p.m.—Queen Mary meets the King at Royal Lodge, Windsor Great Park.
9.0 p.m.—Duke of York arrives back at 145,

Piccadilly. The Prime Minister, Sir John Simon and Mr. Monckton at No. 10. cession of messengers with brief cases
9.15 p.m.—Mr. Malcolm MacDonald at 10.
10.0 p.m.—Sir John Simon and Mr. ton again at No. 10.
10.30 p.m.—Mr. Ramsay MacDonald Colonial Office
11.20 p.m.—Mr. Monckton left No. 1 King's car.

Edward
the Uncrowned

3

FROM A WINDOW in St James's Palace Edward VIII watched the splendid pageantry of his Proclamation. The herald proclaimed it, the people acclaimed it. Never had there been more vociferous joy at the prospect of a new up-to-date king. By his side stood Mrs Simpson. The lady had also watched King George V's Silver Jubilee procession from St James's. But then it was from one of the windows at Major Hardinge's, the King's Assistant Private Secretary. The Prince, who of course was riding in the procession, had arranged for the Hardinges to find room for Wallis and a woman friend under the guise of 'two maids'. This time it was different.

Other differences from the *ancien régime* of George V were soon to strike the Duke and Duchess of York, none of them welcome. Old servants from the royal residences were given notice in the interests of economy, the Duke of York being ordered to wield the axe on behalf of his brother. Bertie had to act entirely through officials. He hardly saw David these days, who preferred to be at Fort Belvedere, his secluded

LEFT *The 'High and Mighty Prince Edward' is proclaimed King-Emperor.*

OPPOSITE *Abdication. The* Daily Mirror *tells of Edward VIII's grim decision.*

*The new King endures the
tedious presentation
ritual of the year's
debutantes in the grounds
of Buckingham Palace.*

home near Virginia Water, rather than at Windsor Castle or
Sandringham. He felt he had lost a friend and perhaps a brother too. No
doubt he and his wife had in their time found a royal residence – White
Lodge – something of a white elephant. Nevertheless it was hurtful that
Edward should now regard the family's beloved Sandringham as
virtually a white elephant also.

The Yorks, however, had not as yet seen the Crown itself falling from
its high place – or only seen it symbolically. The Maltese Cross had been
shaken from the Imperial Crown as it was carried through the streets on
George v's coffin, and had rolled into the gutter. In that cortège, out of six
sovereigns who followed the coffin marched three future abdicators,
King Carol of Roumania, King Leopold III of the Belgians, and King
Edward VIII, and a fourth, King Boris of Bulgaria, whose father had
abdicated in his favour.

It soon became apparent that the new King would economize on time
as well as wages. He decided to receive the Loyal Addresses all together
instead of separately. Nor were the representatives of foreign embassies
allowed the traditional honour of an individual audience. Indeed, the
only embassy he was really interested in was the Embassy Club. In the
words of his own memoirs, *A King's Story*, he preferred an evening with
a few intimates at the Embassy Club or in their homes, to time spent 'in
the great houses or salons of London'. It was a short step from being
allergic to the pleasures of society to being allergic to the duties also. At a
Buckingham Palace garden party he sat under a canopy looking bored,
while outside the rain spattered down and the debutantes queued up.
When they were thoroughly damp and their hats spoilt, he disappeared

indoors ordering the queue to disperse. Thus the last-comers had not even the consolation of making a wet curtsey.

Shortly before that unlucky afternoon, the King said something to Harold Nicolson which suggested that Edward VIII was bored even with his own charm. The King was describing an encounter with the wife of the American aviator, Mrs Anne Lindbergh. Anne had been rather shy at first, said the King, 'but with my well-known charm I put her at ease ...' Such irony, however human, is not reassuring in a king. Though he had begun by performing his royal functions superbly during the early months of his reign, Edward now had other matters on his mind.

The Duchess of York had recovered from her winter's scourge of influenza, but still felt an uncomfortable change in the temperature and atmosphere. At first she thought it was just the loss of her friend the old King. 'I am really very well now,' she wrote to Lord Dawson his doctor in March, 'and I think I am now suffering from the effects of the family break-up – which always happens when the head of a family goes.' But then again it might be something different ... 'Though outwardly one's life goes on the same, yet everything is different – especially spiritually and mentally. I don't know if it is the result of being ill, but I mind things that I don't like more than before.' One of the things she did not like was the new King's obsession.

Mrs Simpson's name on the list of guests at a Buckingham Palace ball had been 'sold' to George V by his eldest son as a means of cultivating Anglo-American friendship. So King George had restored the name that he had previously crossed out and Mrs Simpson duly appeared, but untypically in a 'very showy red dress'. In May 1936 there was another 'showy' display, but this time an entirely characteristic one.

The young King called on his brother and sister-in-law at Royal Lodge, bringing over with him from The Fort two objects for their inspection: his new American station-wagon, and his no less highly polished American friend. 'Who is *she*?' asked Lilibet, sensing an atmosphere of strain, despite her particular fondness for her Uncle David. The '*she*' in question has left a vivid picture of the York family that afternoon: the two little Princesses well-scrubbed and well-mannered, the Duchess with what Mrs Simpson called her 'famous charm' in evidence, and the Duke 'quiet, shy, obviously dubious of this new-fangled American contrivance'. That was a reference to the woman not the wagon, for Mrs Simpson concluded: 'While the Duke of York was sold on the American station-wagon, the Duchess was not sold on David's other American interest.'

Mrs Simpson's proprietary attitude towards the King would have been one trait that grated. She was always trying to cure his bad habits, such as smoking in the wrong places. As Frances Donaldson remarks, who could imagine the discreet Mrs Keppel taking the big cigar out of Edward VII's mouth? Mrs Simpson was well intentioned, but indiscreet to flaunt her proprietorship in public. So obvious had it become that the old Court were quoting a slogan, 'King Edward the Eighth and Mrs Simpson the Seven-eighths'.

Edward VIII and Wallis Simpson photographed together at the fashionable Embassy Club in London.

The young King delighted in his nieces, Elizabeth and Margaret. A photograph taken at Balmoral.

Moreover, on this visit to Royal Lodge Mrs Simpson assumed proprietary airs towards the estate as well as the King. Looking out of the Yorks' drawing-room window, she suggested to the King improvements that might be made in the trees by judicious felling. Of course she genuinely shared the King's interest in gardening, and Royal Lodge belonged to the Crown. But the Yorks were interested in gardening too; and at least for the present it happened to be their garden.

The year before, Mrs Belloc Lowndes, another contemporary diarist, had asked Alexander Woollcott, the famous American broadcaster, whether Edward was really in love with Wallis. Woollcott replied, 'Yes, she has him like *that*.'

'God guide the King!' the Archbishop of Canterbury had written to Queen Mary before the Accession. By the summer of 1936 it had become all too clear who was the King's guide. Chips Channon called him 'Mrs Simpson's absolute slave'.

The Yorks still hoped the whole thing was an aberration and would blow over. Marriage with the already twice-married '*she*' was unthinkable, and hardly to be discussed even among their closest friends. When the irrepressible Winston Churchill tried to draw the Duchess on the subject, she stonewalled heroically. First, Churchill raised the problem of George IV's unconstitutional marriage to Mrs Fitzherbert. To this the Duchess replied, 'That was a long time ago.' Then her wily interlocutor turned to the clash between York and Lancaster during the Wars of the Roses. (Edward VIII was about to go on holiday abroad as 'Duke of Lancaster'.) 'Oh, that was a *very* long time ago,' said the Duchess firmly.

Actually it was as 'Duke of Lancaster' that the King committed one of the great *bêtises* of his reign. In August he hired a yacht, the *Nahlin*, and took Mrs Simpson and a few friends cruising down the Dalmatian coast and in the Mediterranean, without making the slightest attempt to disguise from the delighted crowds and even more enthusiastic press photographers his state of emotional intoxication. By means of the cruise, photographs and gossip about his affair were disseminated throughout America. At home, however, the press were still mum. Two press lords, Beaverbrook and Rothermere, had entered into a 'gentleman's agreement' by which the 'King's Affair', as it had come to be called, should not be mentioned.

A second blunder was committed by him in September at Balmoral. He had earlier refused an invitation from the Lord Provost of Aberdeen to open new hospital buildings in that city, giving as his reason the continuation of Court mourning. (He had not denied himself the pleasures of Ascot week in June, however; nor hesitated to delegate his duty in Aberdeen to the Duke of York.) When the day for the hospital fête arrived, Edward had forgotten everything except that Wallis was arriving too. He drove himself into Aberdeen, was seen picking her up at the station – no signs of mourning, rather the contrary – and blithely carrying her off to Balmoral with all the open panache of a Young Lochinvar. The Scots were deeply shocked.

Various contradictory explanations have been given for this second gross indiscretion. Marie Belloc Lowndes heard that the King had had a chill. Chips Channon, on the other hand, recorded that the King had simply 'chucked' the hospital engagement; while Nigel Nicolson, editor of his father Harold Nicolson's *Diaries*, stated the King pleaded 'a prior engagement'. The number of different stories simply underlines the widespread damage that the thoughtless and besotted King had done to his own cause. A further personal affront was put upon the Duchess of York. Invited over to Balmoral from Birkhall, she found herself the victim of a protocol by which she was the guest of Mrs Simpson. For it was *she*, no less, who came forward to welcome the Duchess and her husband. Mrs Simpson as the successor to Lady Furness was one thing; as the successor to Queen Mary quite another.

But this was precisely the King's intention for her. On 20 October he told the alarmed Prime Minister Mr Baldwin that Mrs Simpson was going to divorce her husband and nothing would stop her. Sure enough, a week later, on the 27th, Mrs Simpson obtained a divorce, the grounds being Ernest Simpson's adultery with a married woman named Mary Kirk Raffray. As this lady subsequently divorced her husband and became Simpson's third wife, the case may have been justified. On the other hand, there seems no reason to believe that Ernest Simpson had turned voluntarily away from Wallis – until he found that this would be an acceptable way out for all concerned. Mary Kirk had been bridesmaid at Wallis Warfield's first marriage to Win Spencer.

Still the royal gossip showed no signs of bursting into the British press. In any case there was plenty of other sensational news to fill the front

During the 'nightmare' weeks before the Abdication, the Duke of York races from his car into 145 Piccadilly, the Yorks' London home.

pages. Mussolini had completed his conquest of Abyssinia early in 1936, civil war had broken out in Spain in July and in September Hitler's Germany invaded the internationalized zone of the Rhineland. Better that public attention should be focused on these signs of the times – signs of war – than on Mrs Simpson's *decree nisi*. Unfortunately this sense of proportion was not to last much longer.

Indeed, there were to be only five weeks between the date of the Simpsons' divorce and the public's sudden discovery of what it meant. Its meaning, in fact, possessed an inexorable logic that uplifted Edward VIII and cast down his family and Government. In six months' time, on 27 April 1937, Mrs Simpson would be free. That would give her and the King just a fortnight in which to get married; for the Coronation was already fixed for 12 May. Edward VIII would be crowned King – and not without his wife by his side. The Government shuddered as the impossible, the absurd picture unfolded itself in their imagination – marriage by the Archbishop of Canterbury in Westminster Abbey, with a solemn communion service and holy oil – emphatically not the mystical setting for a twice-divorced woman with two living ex-husbands.

There were only two courses which would render a traditional Coronation possible. First, Mrs Simpson could renounce the King and go away. As people had once chanted to Caroline of Brunswick:

> But if the effort is too great,
> Go away at any rate.

Alternatively, the King could do as he had threatened to do, marry her and abdicate.

For the Duke and Duchess of York these next five weeks, 27 October to 3 December, were undiluted hell. The Duke's official biographer, Sir

John Wheeler-Bennett, who was not prone to exaggerate, used the expression 'nightmare' three times, and in describing the Duke's feelings sprinkled his narrative with almost the whole vocabulary of anguish: consternation, incredulity, unrelieved gloom; dreaded, tragic, poignant, awful, ghastly; surprised, horrified, appalled.

We can be certain that the Duchess was under no less strain than her husband. True, by temperament she was not a worrier. But hitherto it had been her wifely role to persuade him that the majority of life's little anxieties would retreat if you looked them pleasantly in the face. This, however, was not a small matter. The moment the King abdicated it would be exactly as if he had died: *Vive le Roi* – Long live the King, and no more Duke of York, Duchess of York, Elizabeth or Margaret Rose of York; no more private life. 'Goodbye Piccadilly ...' It had been fun singing the old songs around Lady Strathmore's piano in Bruton Street and around the Duchess's own piano in 145 Piccadilly. This would not be fun.

At this juncture Major Alec Hardinge, newly appointed as the King's Private Secretary, precipitated a further crisis. To understand it, we must look back for a moment. Alec Hardinge had been the first to break the bad news to the Yorks, on their return from Birkhall in October, that Mr Baldwin had been snubbed in an interview with the King on the 20th. Alec's sister, incidentally, was Diamond Hardinge (called after Queen Victoria's Jubilee), a very close friend of the Duchess of York and one of her bridesmaids. Helen Hardinge, Alec's wife, had been born a Cecil. The three families – Salisburys, Strathmores, Hardinges – were country neighbours. They would have seen eye to eye on questions of faith and morals, and would have had no sympathy with the 'Fort set'. Nevertheless Alec Hardinge was absolutely loyal to his master the King.

In the second week of November Major Hardinge consulted Mr Baldwin about the Crown's peril. It was his duty, as secretary, to warn the King. With Baldwin's agreement Hardinge wrote a long letter to His Majesty on the 13th, concluding with two lethal points: 'resignation of the Government' was on the cards, if the King married Mrs Simpson contrary to their advice; the crash could be avoided only if Mrs Simpson went abroad *'without further delay'*.

Now it was the turn of the King to blaze with shock and anger. He refused to answer Hardinge's letter or indeed ever to speak to him again. Instead Edward appointed Walter Monckton as his future liaison with the Government (fortunately an excellent choice) and on the 16th summoned Mr Baldwin to the Palace. The shock was forthwith transmitted to Baldwin. He heard from his King that Edward would either marry Mrs Simpson 'as soon as she is free' or be *'prepared to go'*. Immediately Baldwin went home and straight to bed. It was a measure of his despair.

The family despair was even more poignant when Edward broke the news to them. He told his mother first, going to her that same evening. According to his own account of their meeting, 'The word "duty" fell between us.' If so, it fell stone dead.

Next day Edward similarly informed his three brothers, Bertie, George and Harry. There was no question of Bertie taking to his bed like Baldwin. 'If the worst happens & I have to take over,' he wrote to Godfrey Thomas, the King's Assistant Private Secretary, 'you can be assured that I shall do my best to clear up the inevitable mess...' Then he added as an afterthought, '... if the whole fabric does not crumble under the shock and strain of it all.'

He too was very much part of that shaken royal fabric, so he may have been thinking of himself. But he would have realized in the next breath that all the 'shock and strain' in the world would be powerless against the indomitable combination of himself and his wife. After it was all over, his wife wrote to the Archbishop of Canterbury: 'The curious thing is that we are not afraid.'

Nevertheless, the strain was far from over as November ebbed away. After the King's two excruciating interviews with his family on 17 and 18 November, the Duke of York noted in his diary that he himself had conducted five more interviews between the 18th and 24th, one each with the King and Prime Minister, and three with Queen Mary. The Duke sometimes had to refer to Mrs Simpson in his account, but he could not bring himself to mention her name. She is always 'Mrs ——'.

By now everyone except the general public knew that Mrs Simpson's name was creating a worldwide furore. She herself received hundreds of 'frightful' letters threatening her with death and destruction. She heard the windows next door being broken in mistake for her own, and was personally abused by two women who entered her house as alleged friends. Marie Belloc Lowndes was told that though Mrs Simpson was closely guarded the police could not guarantee her safety. The King was

Edward, grim-faced, shortly before the Abdication.

furious, added Marie Belloc Lowndes, because even some of his own circle would not receive her. Mrs Hannah Gubbay, for instance, the sister of Sir Philip Sassoon, tried to avoid her. They met none the less in Sir Philip's Park Lane mansion. 'Hannah, of course, was there,' wrote Marie, 'and Mrs Simpson was really rude to her, speaking coldly of Hannah's friendship with the Duchess of York.'

Mrs Simpson, miserable and frightened, was persuaded by the King to move over to The Fort, where she could be properly protected. After all, what's a fort for? Meanwhile far-reaching solutions were still being advocated by their friends, who now formed an embryo 'King's Party'. Lord Rothermere urged a morganatic marriage, by which Mrs Simpson would be the King's consort but not his queen. Winston Churchill held out the possibility of a full, constitutional marriage – if only the King would not be in such a hurry. Let him get himself crowned next year and then return to Mrs Simpson when the public had got used to the idea. Patience, only patience . . .

Edward, however, could not stomach a wait of longer than the six months necessary for a decree absolute; and the Dominions could not stomach a morganatic way out at any price.

As the affair rose to its climax, the Yorks were characteristically

In a vain attempt to sway the King's decision, Wallis Simpson made a hasty, but not unnoticed, exit for France.

HM Queen Elizabeth

performing a spell of duty in Scotland. Here the word 'duty' was very much alive. They left London on 29 November, the Duke most unhappy to depart from the scene of action, where he felt that at any moment now he might be drafted to the Throne, 'like the proverbial "sheep being led to the slaughter", which is not a comfortable feeling.' But he had to take his brother's place, vacated on kingship, as Master Mason of Scotland. The Duchess's smiles were particularly brilliant on this tour. It was the best way to hide their wretchedness.

When the Duke and Duchess returned to London on the night of 2 December, the grim secret had come out. 'My heart dropped,' the Duchess said years afterwards, remembering the scene. Euston Station was 'aflame' with lurid posters (to quote Harold Nicolson's diary) which assuredly scorched the unfortunate Yorks. THE KING'S MARRIAGE. THE KING'S MARRIAGE.

The Duke hurried round to Queen Mary, who had become a stately lighthouse in a stormy sea. At one point she was so outraged that she burst out to Baldwin, 'Really – this might be Roumania!' (Crown Prince Carol of Roumania had renounced the throne in 1915 in order to pursue his mistress Madame Lupescu. He was back as king in 1929 and abdicated again in 1940.)

Why had it all come out so suddenly, the Duke asked his mother. The answer was that the publication of the 'Mrs ——' crisis had been accidental, and yet at the same time inevitable.

The Bishop of Bradford, Dr Blunt, had spiced a 'Recall to Religion' address with a reminder that the King himself needed God's aid and should step up his church-going. The provincial press mistook this mild rebuke for a denunciation of the 'King's Affair'. All the papers copied. So the cat was out of the bag, as the Duchess of York had once said of her own engagement, 'and nothing in the world could stuff it back.'

That evening of 3 December Mrs Simpson slipped away to Cannes, to escape the press hubbub, and the Duke of York reported in his diary another 'dreadful announcement' to the family by his brother: '(in Mary's & my presence) David said to Queen Mary that he could not live alone as king & must marry Mrs ——.' The King's last words to the Duke, as he left for The Fort that night, were that his brother should come and see him next morning, Friday 4 December.

Now began a truly abysmal week for the Yorks. The Duke waited and waited with his wife at Royal Lodge for the summons from The Fort that never seemed to come. The King put off Friday's appointment to Saturday – to Sunday – to Monday ... The Duke kept telephoning, the King kept stalling. At last on Monday the 7th the Duke went to The Fort for dinner (though invited for *after* dinner only). Into his diary he breathed a great sigh of relief: 'The awful & ghastly suspense of waiting was over.' 'I went back to London that night with my wife,' concluded the Duke. They both knew it was Abdication.

The last days of the Abdication crisis are too well known to merit another re-run in slow motion. In any case, this is the story of Queen Elizabeth the Queen Mother, and she, poor lady, was now only able to follow events from a pile of pillows in Piccadilly. After the stress and strain of the Scottish journey, conducted in mid-winter in secret anxiety, the Duchess succumbed to acute influenza. 'Too unlucky,' wrote Queen Mary. Miserably alone, the Duchess lay at 145 Piccadilly while her husband did what had to be done at Royal Lodge and The Fort.

There was a dinner at Royal Lodge on the 8th, when all were mournful except the King, whom his brother described as 'the life & soul of the party ... & this is the man we are going to lose.' While motoring back and forth between London and Windsor, the Duke had plenty of time to devise new ways of persuading his brother to stay. He tried yet again on the 9th. No use. After reporting this final failure to his mother, he wrote in his diary, 'I broke down & sobbed like a child.' Queen Mary took up the story. 'It is a terrible blow to us all and particularly to poor Bertie.' And all because David wants to marry Mrs Simpson!!!!!'

The Instrument of Abdication was produced at The Fort next day, 10 December. 'Perfectly calm D signed,' wrote his brother. The Duke himself, however, sensed the tension at The Fort and went over to Royal Lodge, to rest. 'But I could not rest alone—'

HM King George VI.

There was sadness and irony in that word 'alone'. The King had already told his family that 'he could not live alone' apart from Mrs Simpson, and he was virtually to repeat those words in his Abdication broadcast. At the moment, no doubt, his brother was having to face it out 'alone' because of the Duchess's temporary illness. But in the years to come, as a result of Edward VIII's decision, they would see less of each other and less of their children than destiny had seemed to promise them when they married thirteen years before. For, as Tennyson had once written for Queen Victoria, they would henceforth stand in 'that fierce light which beats upon a throne' — a light which creates its own loneliness.

The Duke of York (Duke for only a few hours longer) returned to his wife on the evening of the 10th: 'I found a large crowd outside my house cheering madly,' he wrote. 'I was overwhelmed.' Next day the Abdication Bill was given its third reading and royal assent in Parliament at 2.00 p.m. It was Edward VIII's last act as King.

The horizon was beginning to lighten for the family at 145 Piccadilly and for the nation. 'Now if someone comes through on the telephone,' joked the new King to his assembled family at luncheon, 'who should I say I am?' In Parliament someone was already asking about the date of the Coronation. The occasion merited an epigrammatic reply: 'Same day. New King.'

That evening came the Abdication broadcast and the parting of the brothers at Windsor.

King George VI met his Privy Council on 12 December. The hesitations in his speech had returned under stress and his boyish look had changed into a drawn pallor. But what he had to say was good in itself and effectively echoed his brother's broadcast in a more positive sense. 'With my wife and helpmeet by my side,' he said, 'I take up the heavy task which lies before me.'

Queen Consort

4

A QUEEN CONSORT stands in some sense halfway between a Queen Regnant and a Prince Consort. She is not part of the constitution and has no place in it, unlike a Queen who rules in her own right. But whereas a Prince Consort is not crowned along with his wife, the Queen Consort looks forward to her Coronation in the same way as her husband.

Only five short months were to pass between Queen Elizabeth's Accession and her Coronation. The customary span was over a year. Thus as usual a new life was opening out before Queen Elizabeth more rapidly than could have been expected. How strange that the girl who had hesitated before undertaking the responsibilities of a royal duchess should within fourteen years herself succeed to the throne and be crowned Queen almost at one bound.

Because all had already been put in train for Edward VIII's Coronation on 12 May 1937, it seemed advisable not to create yet another upheaval by postponing the date of George VI's. For George VI it was to be, not Albert I. He had been called 'Bertie', short for Albert, all his life, and it might have been thought that Queen Victoria's cherished dream of a 'King Albert' would at last be realized. But Albert sounded more like the Royal Family of Belgium or Monaco, whereas George reminded people of George V and established continuity.

Continuity was what the new King and Queen needed above all. King George VI had been carried to the throne on the wings of a destructive emotional storm. He had vowed to 'make amends' for wounds inflicted on the Crown by the Abdication. But for several days afterwards it was clear that it was he personally, rather than the Crown, that had been severely wounded. His official biographer again uses the strongest possible words to convey his sufferings: 'shock' and emotional disturbance followed by 'numbness'. Both King George VI and his mother Queen Mary have described how he broke down in her presence. A similar breakdown has been recorded by the King's cousin, Lord Louis Mountbatten. 'Dickie, this is absolutely terrible; I'm quite unprepared for it,' the King burst out. 'David has been trained for this all his life. I've never even seen a State Paper. I'm only a naval officer, it's the only thing I know about.' Mountbatten, himself a naval officer, promptly replied, 'There is no finer training for a King.'

Helpful though that answer was, it could not in itself solve the problem of the King's self-depreciation. Perhaps when the Royal Archives are opened, we shall know how the young Queen also expressed her faith in

OPPOSITE *The State portrait of Queen Elizabeth wearing her Coronation robes by Sir Gerald Kelly.*

Shocked and drawn, the new King leaves 145 Piccadilly to take the Oath of Allegiance at St James's Palace, 12 December 1936.

him and, no doubt, her indignation with the forces that had brought him such misery. For the present one thing is certain. The new King's agonized reaction stemmed from a double mistake made in all humility: underestimation of himself and overestimation of his brother.

On the first point, many factors had contributed to undermine his confidence. A proposal, for instance, that he should be Governor-General of Canada had been vetoed by George V and his Ministers. Looking back, one realizes how great a chance had been lost, particularly as the Duchess of York would have shone from the viceregal throne.

There is no evidence, however, that Mr Baldwin actually entertained an idea of superseding the Duke of York by his younger brother, Prince George, Duke of Kent. It was apparently believed by Dermot Morragh (that dedicated interpreter of royalty) that Edward VIII's refusal to see his brother Bertie between 4 and 7 December was due to Baldwin's intervention. Baldwin is said to have canvassed the claims of the younger royal brother George, both as a public speaker and as the father of a male heir. Again only the Royal Archives will be able to settle this rumour one way or the other; though it is now common knowledge (and has appeared in print) that Prince George had had difficulties of his own with

*Three Kings of England:
From the left, Edward VIII,
George V and George VI.
A historic study of George
V and his elder sons
dressed in Air Force
uniform, 1935.*

David   G.R.I.   Bertie
July 6ᵗʰ 1935.

drugs – which would seem to cast extreme doubt on the whole story.

On the second point, it is true that George V had misguidedly withheld all State papers from his younger son. Therefore George VI's complaint that he had 'never even seen a State Paper' was an incontrovertible fact. Moreover, we are informed by his official biographer that George VI was 'appalled' by the number of red dispatch-boxes, when he did see them. His conscientiousness, on the other hand, made him more and more master of his new duties. Edward VIII, by way of contrast, had given less and less time to the royal boxes, so absorbed was he in his love affair.

George VI had idolized his brother since boyhood. By 1936 he had come to exaggerate Edward's aptitude for monarchy. Edward had facility and charm, certainly; though even the charm could be switched off and the whole personality plunged into a melancholy half-light. An older woman once said of the Prince: 'That boy puzzles me. He's so absolutely full of life, and yet at times he has a look in his eyes that haunts me ... A tragic look, a sort of destiny look.' All this was written and published years before Mrs Simpson appeared on the scene.

Lord Mountbatten remembered that 'the responsibilities of being Prince of Wales sometimes weighed heavily on him', and Edward 'often expressed the wish that he could exchange places' with his ebullient cousin, Dickie. A wish to exchange places with his brother Bertie had apparently been lodged somewhere at the back of Edward's mind at least since 1935. Edward had shown hysterical grief at King George V's death, and this evoked surprise. It is now thought to have been due to despair at having missed his cue and failed to renounce the kingship while his father was still alive. An equerry, Major Verney, noticed Edward's revolt against 'the deadening inevitability of his destiny', the 'subtle appeal of uncertainty' and the 'lure of a mysterious future'; his need to gamble with life, take chances, take risks. 'His composition screams for it.'

In the light of such an analysis, Edward's attempt both to marry Mrs Simpson *and* to make her Queen may be regarded as his last and supreme gamble – the throw that failed.

The 'composition' of George VI always had more ballast. Yet in every respect he had felt himself the inferior. (In fact he was a far better all-round athlete.) The brothers shared many high qualities, including concern with youth and industrial welfare. Each could fall into fits of depression or acute irritation. But the younger brother, despite his early ill-health, remained the more stable of the two. King George VI had a useful dash of his father's conservatism together with his mother's interest in things new.

It seems highly likely that Queen Elizabeth had long ago made a realistic assessment of the two brothers on these lines. Her mission, however, was not to criticize her brother-in-law but to 'advise, encourage and warn' her husband. I have chosen that famous phrase precisely because it embodies the duty of a monarch towards his Ministers, as defined by Walter Bagehot, the celebrated nineteenth-century royal observer. By way of analogy, a Queen Consort's duty towards the Sovereign her husband may be seen as the same. The King's to initiate and decide within the partnership; the Queen's to support in the fullest sense.

There were indeed early signs that the King knew his own mind. On Friday 11 December ('Abdication Day') he saw the Lord Chancellor's representative about Edward's future title. 'I suggest HRH Duke of Windsor,' said King George firmly.

A 'spell-binding Queen' was how Lady Diana Cooper had described Queen Elizabeth on her accession. The Queen would need to weave more than one spell if the run-up to the Coronation were to pass smoothly. Buckingham Palace had to be changed somehow from a vast habitation of ghosts into a home. Edward VIII had totally neglected its six hundred rooms, concentrating all his money and imagination on Fort Belvedere. The two little Princesses would undoubtedly have preferred to have remained at 145 Piccadilly, and there were plans to make a secret underground passage between Buckingham Palace and their real 'home'. As their father had once said, 'Just like the Middle Ages . . .'.

But Queen Elizabeth succeeded in dragging at least part of Buckingham Palace into the twentieth century, with the minimum of new carpets and curtains in the rooms they actually used, and the maximum of flowers. It was no time for lavish decorating, what with an economic depression that seemed endless and a worsening international situation. A family atmosphere costs nothing; and in Queen Elizabeth the Royal Family at last acquired a creative artist in home life. Perhaps for the first time since the Stuarts the Royal Family were now completely united and at ease with one another. Queen Victoria always had reservations about children, while Edward VII and George V chafed their sons too much for comfort, causing tongue-tied silences.

Queen Elizabeth, as one of her first acts, abolished the old, stilted custom of royal children curtseying to their parents. Henceforth each morning the Princesses could fly down the long corridors to greet their parents without stopping at the last minute to bend the knee. The curtseys were reserved for their grandmother Queen Mary.

Lady Diana Cooper has left us a vivacious sketch of life at Windsor Castle in April 1937. She and her husband, Duff Cooper (then Secretary of State for War), had been invited for the night of the 16th. Everything in their suite was still Victorian; the 'good' coal fire, piano, 'well-stocked writing-tables', tapless bath 'lidded in mahogany' for Duff, 'throttlingly-stuffy' bedroom with 'a bed for three', another huge bathroom with a 'loo' and everywhere innumerable oil paintings, plaques, miniatures, wax profiles and bronzes of the old Royal Family.

Lady Diana was told by Alec Hardinge (now once more serving his King) that it would be 'Good night' at 10.30 p.m. But the Queen – 'in gloss of satin, a lily and rose in one' – sent for Duff as her Minister, and Diana was writing in her diary in mock envy after midnight: 'He came back at 12.30. One hour so-called tea-drinking with the Queen.' The Queen had put her feet up on a sofa and talked of kingship and 'the intolerable honour'. She did not mention the Abdication crisis. 'Shan't write any more,' ended Lady Diana. 'Too tired. Duff so happy, me rather piqued.'

The Coronation demanded of the Queen beautiful dresses to gladden the people's hearts. Queen Elizabeth was not in the least vain or self-conscious about thinking in terms of beauty and magnificence. The portrait-painter John Sargent once described her, when still a very young Duchess, as 'The only completely unselfconscious sitter I have ever had.' After the Abdication she had promised Queen Mary to make the best of her new role, unwanted though it was. A Coronation has two aspects, religious and spectacular. Queen Elizabeth saw it as her plain duty to make the most of both.

On 11 May, the evening before the Coronation, the King and Queen received a visit from the Archbishop of Canterbury. This was forgiving, since in his abdication broadcast the Archbishop had unwisely attempted to smooth King George's path by warning the public about the pauses in his speech. The Archbishop's own fluency on the subject had caused more surprise than the pauses themselves. During the last few weeks the Queen had been helping her husband to practise the breathing for his responses in the Abbey.

At the Palace the Archbishop now explained to the King and Queen

RIGHT *Sir Gerald Kelly's State portrait of King George VI. The King wears his Coronation robes and holds the sceptre. On a cushion to the right is set the Imperial State Crown.*

BELOW *A scene inside Westminster Abbey during the Coronation of the King.*

CC 16

ABOVE *Attended by their pages and maids-of-honour, the King and Queen stand on the balcony of Buckingham Palace with their two daughters. Queen Mary acknowledges the response of the crowds.*

LEFT *A souvenir postcard of the Coronation of King George VI and Queen Elizabeth, 12 May 1937, bearing part of the King's message of thanks to his peoples.*

SOUVENIR

MAY 12th
1937
G R
VI

"THE QUEEN & I WILL ALWAYS KEEP WITHIN OUR HEARTS THE INSPIRATION OF THIS DAY" FROM THE KINGS BROADCAST 12TH MAY

THE KING'S PROCESSION

the sacred and self-dedicatory aspect of their Coronation, and together they prayed. The eve of the ceremony thus became something of a vigil in the medieval sense.

With characteristic sensitivity to the feelings of others, Queen Elizabeth stuck to her rather old-fashioned Court dressmaker for the Coronation robes. The worthy Mme Handley Seymour would have been heart-broken to be superseded on this day of all days. So the Queen's Coronation robe was traditional, indeed it was very like the robe Queen Mary wore in 1911, which in turn closely resembled Queen Alexandra's in 1902: purple velvet with ermine shoulder-cape, ermine borders and a train with rounded ends, but lined for Queen Elizabeth with white satin instead of fur. (Queen Alexandra had had hers lined with rabbit instead of ermine to save expense.) The velvet was embroidered in gold thread with symbols of the British Empire – the rose, thistle, shamrock, leek, maple, fern, mimosa and lotus. There was also one Imperial Crown with two interlaced 'E's'. Queen Mary's robe had borne the Crown and letter 'M', while Queen Alexandra's had a scattering of small crowns at all angles, some upside down, as if to foreshadow those that would topple in the next decade.

Queen Elizabeth's dress was of white satin cut on the cross, according to the thirties fashion, and again embroidered with national emblems in glittering diamanté. The Queen's personal choice showed in her white satin shoes with their high heels – a style from which she never deviated – and adorned with oak leaves and thistles of England and Scotland in gold thread. They were made by Jack Jacobus of Shaftesbury Avenue, where the most modern shoes were sold. The 'brightest jewel in her crown', however, was the age-old, historic Koh-i-Noor diamond – 'Mountain of Light' – presented to Queen Victoria by the East India Company when the Punjab was annexed in 1849.

If the Queen's Coronation dress necessarily lacked the stylish novelty of Princess Marina's with its fawn lamé, feather pattern picked out in rhinestones and its breakaway from bias cutting, the Queen's own ideas were already moving towards a new dressmaker, Norman Hartnell. He had designed exquisite stage creations. Now the Queen asked him to present some ideas for her maids-of-honour at the Coronation. The Queen's lifelong interest in history had inspired her to look up the patterns used for Queen Victoria's maids-of-honour. She suggested to Hartnell the Victorian motif of wheat-ears.

Hartnell has left an affectionate description of the Duchess of York and her daughters on their first visit to his salon. The Duchess in silver-grey georgette, the children in silver-buttoned blue jackets and with forget-me-knots on their tiny grey hats, formed 'a symphony of silver and blue'. As Hartnell conducted the royal party through the salon, he noticed the Duchess's special dignity: 'With lovely smile and gracious movement the Duchess of York acknowledged on either side the reverences of the women present and very slowly moved on and out of sight.'

So the great day of the Coronation arrived. The King was woken at

3.00 a.m. by loudspeakers being tested. It would have been a severe enough test for any human being, even without the King's sensitive nervous system. No wonder he had 'a sinking feeling' and could eat no breakfast. By 10.00 a.m. the suspense was over at last, and Their Majesties left the Palace for the Abbey in the golden coach, accompanied by all the panoply of state. The enormous State coach was a mass of carved gilded foliage, twining around panels that had been painted in the eighteenth century by the courtly Italian artist Cipriani, who lay buried in Chelsea. This baroque equipage, with its airborne gods and goddesses upholding the crown while cherubs blew encouraging blasts on their trumpets, contrasted strangely with the dedicated pair who sat inside: His Majesty's expression calm but still a little tense; Her Majesty's charmingly open face always, it seemed, about to break into smiles.

The King's tenseness was justified by the number of things that went wrong, as indeed they do at most Coronations. A whole generation usually separates these historic events, so that there are plenty of opportunities for age and inexperience to cause mistakes. Old men miss steps and roll over; people faint. In this case it was one of the chaplains, who thereby held up the Queen's procession – and small wonder, since the chaplains were subjected to interminable standing and were clad up to the neck and down to the toes in long thick cloaks of scarlet woollen cloth, lined with white silk and fastened at the throat with red and white cord. Then the King's white surplice or Colobium Sindonis was offered to him inside out; the place lost in one holy book and another presented with the relevant passage covered; the Crown probably put on the wrong way round; and the King himself momentarily pinned to the ground by a bishop standing on his robe. 'I had to tell him to get off it pretty smartly as I nearly fell down.'

For Queen Elizabeth the emotions could flow uninterrupted. No one could imagine the experience, she was to say afterwards, and once you had been through it you never felt the same again. There were no chattering maids-of-honour, as there had been at Queen Victoria's Coronation, to disturb her act of total commitment to God and her country. If there was any whispering, it came from Queen Elizabeth's two charming young daughters, both dressed in long white lace dresses with gold bows down the front, subtly reminiscent of what the seven-year-old Elizabeth Bowes-Lyon used to wear, though the necks of the Princesses' dresses were round not square. The Queen herself, however, had chosen a square neck, and the heads of roses and thistles were embroidered in a row down the front.

The Princesses Elizabeth and Margaret, now aged just eleven and six-and-a-half, wore purple robes that were miniature editions of their grandmother Queen Mary's robe, when she was Princess of Wales at Edward VII's Coronation in 1902. But there were two innovations to highlight the family's unity. The first was the presence of Queen Mary herself, wearing the very robe of 1902 from which the little Princesses' versions had been copied. This was the first time a Queen Dowager had attended the Coronation of her successor, an indication of family solidarity.

*'Alas, wedding-day'
Queen Mary noted in her
diary on 3 June 1937, as
the recently created Duke
of Windsor and Mrs
Wallis Warfield Simpson
were married in France.*

The other innovation was the presence of the two royal children. It seemed to bring out the truth of Edward VIII's words at his abdication, when he lamented his own lack of family and emphasized his brother's good fortune. 'And he has one matchless blessing . . . not bestowed on me – a happy home life with his children.' The presence of Princess Elizabeth, however, was probably due to her mother's view that such a historic event was part of her education in the highest sense. Princess Margaret is said to have urgently insisted on going too.

Another trusty supporter was the Queen's friend old Lady Airlie, wearing again the crimson velvet with ermine tails she had worn in 1911 at King George V's Coronation. All these historic robes and dresses are now in the Museum of London – as is that of the Countess of Dudley, formerly Gertie Millar the chorus girl, who was there in the Abbey with the peeresses, raising her white arms to put on her coronet and salute the crowned King. It must have been puzzling for Mrs Simpson when she read about it: if Gertie Millar could be there as a countess, why not Wallis Warfield as a queen?

King George VI and Queen Elizabeth, anointed and crowned, drove through miles of umbrellas and people joyful despite the rain, before they at length returned to the Palace. Once more, as after their wedding, they were both uplifted and tired out. But whereas it was the King who confessed to a 'sinking feeling' at the start, it was the Queen who actually sank exhausted at the close. She had completely lost her voice. Yet next day they were out again, driving around London's East End, a poignant foreshadowing of the Queen's visits during the blitz, when the bombing of her own palace enabled her to 'look the East End in the face'.

By 27 May 1937 King George was ready with an important statement for his brother the Duke of Windsor. The Royal Family had heard that Edward and Mrs Simpson were to be married in France on 3 June. 'Alas, wedding-day,' Queen Mary would write in her diary. 'Alas, birthday,' she might also have written, for 3 June was King George v's, and it seemed to her a particularly tasteless date to choose for Mrs Simpson's third nuptials. Indeed, it had become a semi-sacred date. King George v had made Queen Mary a Garter Lady on his birthday and, in the words of Queen Elizabeth, 'the coincidence was so charming' that King George vi had made his wife a Garter Lady on his own birthday also. The Simpson wedding-day coincidence was not 'so charming'.

The Royal Family had to look to the future. Exactly a week before the wedding, the style and title of the Duke of Windsor and of his future wife were given legal form. By Letters Patent, issued under the Lord Chancellor's Seal, the Duke was 'entitled to hold and enjoy for himself only the title style or attribute of Royal Highness so however that his wife and descendants if any shall not hold the said title style or attribute.' On receiving this unwelcome news the Duke burst out, 'What a *damnable* wedding-present!' and ever since that moment an argument has raged about the validity of the King's decision. By what right, asked the Windsors' partisans, did His Majesty deny the Duchess of Windsor the same rank as her husband, namely, the avidly desired HRH?

The first answer must be that she had no automatic legal claim. The title of HRH must be created by Letters Patent – and if the Letters Patent say no, no it is. The second answer depends upon an overall judgment as to what was best for the country at the time. The Abdication had momentarily shaken the Monarchy, and any further upheavals were to be avoided. So the possible instability of the Windsors' marriage was one consideration. According to Mrs Belloc Lowndes, even Winston Churchill himself, the 'King's man', said to her at a New Year's dinner in 1937, 'He [Edward] falls constantly in and out of love. His present attachment will follow the course of all the others.' Would it last? Mrs Simpson had been married now three times. If she divorced her third husband also – and even a fourth – nothing would divorce her from the HRH, once bestowed. The Commonwealth countries in particular shied away from the idea of a floating HRH, so to speak, detached from the Royal Family. When the New Zealand Premier heard that Wallis Windsor would be only 'Her Grace', his comment was, 'And quite enough too.'

The British Government were in two minds about Edward's future.

Some were for his remaining abroad, others for his coming home to lend a hand. When it became clear, however, that Edward would not return to Britain without his wife and his wife's royal title, the situation was further bedevilled.

The writer Alastair Forbes, in the *Times Literary Supplement* (4 January 1980), described an early symptom of this new trouble. Queen Mary instructed Princess Marina in June 1937 not to call on the Duchess of Windsor with her husband Prince George of Kent. 'Marina (being a foreigner by birth) shouldn't be the first female member of the family to call on her, as the feeling against the Duchess of Windsor in England was very strong.' As a result the Duke of Windsor told his brother George not to come either.

The entry of Queen Mary into the picture introduces at least one fixed point. She never would and never did receive Mrs Simpson – except with five exclamation marks in the pages of her diary, and in her coffin at her funeral. But if faced with *HRH* the Duchess of Windsor, there would have been no escape even for Queen Mary. It has been said that all the royal ladies, including Queen Elizabeth, took precisely the same line as Queen Mary. This can only be true for Queen Mary's lifetime, since all the royal ladies, including Queen Elizabeth the Queen Mother and Queen Elizabeth II, received the Windsors at the unveiling of the memorial to Queen Mary – in itself a curious touch of irony.

Nevertheless, every so often the popular press, sparked off by ephemera such as the television film *Edward and Mrs Simpson*, wonder why 'our beloved warm-hearted Queen Mum' should have proved so 'unrelenting', so 'unforgiving' towards the Duchess of Windsor. This question must be examined.

During the first three years of their reign the new King and Queen felt a real sense of insecurity. How would the country take *us*? they asked themselves. No prince had ever been more popular than Edward, and their own style by comparison was quiet and unassuming. It was not beyond the bounds of possibility that the Windsors should stage a come-back – or so it seemed in those troubled early days. Edward himself had decided, 'No HRH for Wallis, no home-coming for me.' Was this altogether a disaster?

Queen Elizabeth had devoted herself to her husband's development and happiness over the past fourteen years. Suddenly it was all to be put in jeopardy. His anguished reaction to the Abdication crisis showed how deeply he could suffer from any clash with his adored elder brother. Illogically, he may even have felt the guilt of a usurper – though a profoundly reluctant one. As late as mid-1939, Mrs Belloc Lowndes heard that 'The King constantly talks of his brother: it is as if he can't think of anything else; he seems haunted by him.' How could the Court and country ever 'settle down' (to use George v's favourite phrase) if Edward were constantly to flash across the sky like a shooting star with a glittering tail? In the interest of her family, her husband and his people, the firm line taken by the Queen was justified, and any other wife of equal character would have hoped to do likewise.

OPPOSITE *On the day after their Coronation, King George and Queen Elizabeth toured their capital city. Crowds surged around the royal Daimler in London's East End.*

Fortunately or otherwise, Edward's own attitude and behaviour quickly proved the impossibility of having him home. He telephoned his brother from abroad almost daily with advice, criticism and complaints about money. Walter Monckton had to intervene and stop the calls. Moreover, the Windsors were eventually to accept tax-free hospitality from the generous French public. This in fact made sure that they would never choose to live in England, where their circumstances could not be anything like as luxurious. Thus the withholding of the HRH came to serve a dual purpose. It enabled the Windsors to keep up what amounted to a bluff of martyrdom, while living sophisticated and prosperous lives in Paris. And it provided a shield behind which the new royal line could develop in undisturbed harmony.

And the British public? A common friend of both the Royal Family and the Windsors was once asked by Wallis in the south of France: 'Why do the King and Queen treat us as they do?' Her friend replied: 'The public would not allow them to behave in any other way.' She said, 'Yes, I quite understand.' Shortly afterwards the same friend, finding himself alone on the Scottish moors with King George VI, decided to tell him the story. The King simply said, 'Yes, that's right.'

Meanwhile the Windsors were not the only, or even a major problem on the Continent – except in so far as they gave aid and comfort to the Nazis by paying Hitler a visit in October 1937. The next month the King and Queen encouraged the democracies by receiving the Belgian Monarchs on a State visit.

Three months later, on 21 February 1938, Neville Chamberlain's policy of 'appeasing' the dictators was dramatically challenged. Anthony Eden resigned as Foreign Secretary. 'Yesterday was a terrible day,' wrote Harold Nicolson on the 22nd. 'The papers blazed with Anthony's resignation.' The King and Queen did not blaze. They sympathized with Appeasement, believing it to be a true olive branch; but when Eden handed in his seals of office, the King expressed admiration at any rate for his courage. Less than a month later Appeasement produced one of its poisoned fruits. 'A sense of danger and anxiety hangs over us like a pall,' wrote Nicolson. 'Hitler has completely collared Austria . . .'.

That summer it fell to Their Majesties' lot to help promote the Prime Minister's peace policy in Europe. They undertook a State visit to Paris. Its object was both to increase support and understanding for our French ally, and to demonstrate the strength of Britain in her new Sovereigns. The sudden death of the Queen's mother, Lady Strathmore, on 28 June seemed to be a sad augury for the visit. The royal departure was postponed until 19 July. But Queen Elizabeth's brave decision not to do what might be called 'a Queen Victoria', and allow mourning to take precedence over living, brought a splendid reward. The visit was an incomparable success, partly through the very mourning which others might have used as an excuse for not going.

The Queen's new dressmaker, Normal Hartnell, had originally devised a brilliant trousseau, vibrating with colour, for the State visit. He has told in his memoirs, *Silver and Gold*, how the 'French fun' of

Received by Hitler, the Duke and Duchess of Windsor 'gave aid and comfort to the Nazis'. October 1937. A picture which, when published, shocked the British people.

eighteenth-century painters like Watteau and Fragonard had hitherto inspired him. Then one day King George VI took him into the Long Gallery at Buckingham Palace and showed him the royal collection of nineteenth-century Winterhalters, especially the Empresses Eugénie of the French and Elizabeth of Austria. Both wore crinolines. Hartnell at once took the hint. For King George had made it clear that Hartnell should 'capture this picturesque grace' in the dresses he designed for the Queen. If the Empress Eugénie had first introduced the crinoline, it was Queen Elizabeth who would bring it back. The style was made for her: romantic, swaying, swirling. Alas, the wearing of mourning meant that the Queen would have to abandon the whole glowing collection from the house of Hartnell. Did it also mean that she would try to dazzle Paris, if at all, in purple and black?

'Is not white a royal prerogative for mourning, Your Majesty?' Hartnell suggested to the King, perhaps remembering that Queen Victoria after all had insisted on a white funeral. Why not a white State visit? White it would be, decided the Palace. In the fortnight that remained before departure, Hartnell waved a wand over every item of his collection and the whole was reproduced in pure white and more lovely than ever.

They crossed to France in the royal yacht *Enchantress*. A month later the Duff Coopers (he was First Lord of the Admiralty) found the ship still buzzing with Queen Elizabeth's impact. 'The Queen has nobbled everyone,' wrote Lady Diana, from the Commander-in-Chief to a marine. The First Lieutenant was like a lovesick knight-at-arms. Lady Diana doubted if he would ever cast it off.

At the Elysée Palace they were given two bathrooms, one of silver and one of gold, decorated with mosaics, crystal and 'fiddle-de-dees rampant'. During the occupation, Goering was to fill what had been the King's dressing-room with cupboards for a hundred uniforms.

Paris went mad over the Queen's trousseau, a perfect expression of her temperament and beauty. At the Bagatelle garden party her white dress of cobweb lace and tulle trailed like thistledown on the green grass, while the feathers on her sweeping hat dipped in unison. There was a sensation when she opened her gossamer parasol while watching a ballet by the lakeside; she might have been part of the ballet herself.

'We saw the King and Queen from a window,' wrote Lady Diana Cooper, 'coming down the Champs Elysées with roofs, windows and pavements roaring exultantly, the Queen a radiant Winterhalter', but, as the Duff Coopers considered, guarded by the French with 'too many security measures'. These, however, were reduced as popular acclaim grew. (A year later, in Canada, Their Majesties were themselves to make sure of mingling with the people.)

Each night's flourish outdid the last [continued Lady Diana]. At the Opera we leant over the balustrade to see the Royal couple, shining with stars and diadem and the Légion d'Honneur proudly worn, walk up the marble stairs preceded by *les chandeliers* – two valets bearing twenty-branched candelabra of tall white candles.

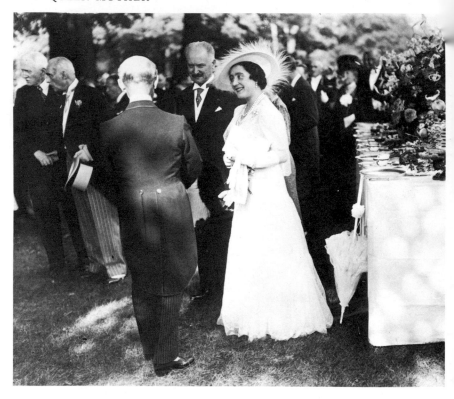

Queen Elizabeth at the Bagatelle garden party during the State visit to Paris in July 1938. As the visit followed shortly after the death of her mother, the Queen reinstated the royal custom of wearing white while in mourning, and took an all white trousseau.

Before the reception in the Elysée Palace, the Queen and her husband sent for Hartnell to thank him for the pleasure his creations had given. 'Please have a glass of champagne before you leave,' said the Queen. 'It is very good champagne, I assure you,' added the King with his delightful simplicity. Even the very best French champagne could not be too good for this King and Queen. For four days France was a Monarchy again. 'We have taken the Queen to our hearts,' announced the French press. 'She rules over two nations.'

The Queen had noticed one macabre touch. During a concert in a chapel, there was a fly-past of fighting planes which ever and again drowned the music and darkened the chapel walls with the shadow of their wings. Within months that dark roar proved to be a better forecast of the future than the lights and laughter.

By September of the same year Hitler's carefully staged destruction of Czechoslovakia had made war all but inevitable. Suddenly Neville Chamberlain's dash to Munich seemed to win a respite, if not 'Peace for our Time'. Millions of British families rejoiced, including the deeply anxious family at Buckingham Palace. The King invited Chamberlain to stand beside the Queen and himself on the Palace balcony, to receive the people's plaudits. Many cried with relief. The King had always liked and understood Chamberlain. Now his faith seemed gloriously justified.

Looking at the photographs of that famous trio on the balcony, one cannot but notice the strangely symmetrical pattern woven by history.

Both the King and his Prime Minister were shy and withdrawn by nature, each having been put in the shade during youth by a charming and outstanding elder brother: in one case Edward, Prince of Wales, in the other Sir Austen Chamberlain. Each of them had been drawn out and inspired by a beautiful and outgoing wife.

Perhaps that partly accounted for the King's loyal friendship with his disastrously unfortunate Premier. Disaster was indeed not far off. It was weeks rather than months before 'Peace for our Time' had become a mockery. Hitler turned the heat on Poland and gobbled up the remains of Czechoslovakia. On 15 March 1939 the Germans occupied Prague. From its ancient Hradschin Castle, built by the kings of Bohemia, Hitler declared: 'Czechoslovakia has ceased to exist.'

The British were arming, but still hastening slowly, and expressing their feelings in characteristic understatements. 'Well, Gibson, and what do you think about Hitler?' the Duke of Devonshire asked his chauffeur one day. 'Well, your Grace,' replied this Derbyshire worthy, 'it seems to me that he should know by now that he is none too popular in this district.' There was no panic. So little, indeed, that the Government considered it perfectly safe to send their King and Queen across the Atlantic on 5 May to Canada and the United States. While Hitler was hammering at the Polish Corridor in the East, Their Majesties should try to open the corridors of power and friendship in the West.

Taking a photograph from the deck of the liner Empress of Australia.

'I hate leaving here,' King George wrote to his mother, 'with the situation as it is.' He improved the situation as far as possible by refusing to sail in the battleship *Repulse*. He and the Queen would sail instead in the liner *Empress of Australia*. The battle fleet should not be short of a key ship because of them.

Their voyage was an unexpected nightmare. Queen Elizabeth's description to Queen Mary of her feelings is so vivid that this example of her liveliness as a letter-writer must be quoted at some length.

For three & a half days we only moved a few miles. The fog was so thick, that it was like a white cloud round the ship, and the fog horn blew incessantly. Its melancholy blasts were echoed by the icebergs like the twang of a piece of wire. Incredibly eery, and really very alarming ... We very nearly hit a berg the day before yesterday, and the poor Captain was nearly demented because some kind cheerful people kept on reminding him that it was about here that the Titanic was struck, & *just* about the same date! ...

It seemed a better omen when the purser's canary laid an egg.

'Wasn't it terrible?' asked a lady-in-waiting many years later. 'Yes it was,' replied Queen Elizabeth the Queen Mother, as she had become. 'You see, we lost two days of the tour.'

This was the first ever royal visit to Canada by a Sovereign and his Consort. It was an overwhelming success, creating a fervour of loyalty and dispersing any whiffs of isolationism or neutralism. The Governor-General, Lord Tweedsmuir (novelist John Buchan), noted that the Queen had 'a perfect genius for the right kind of publicity'. She broke away to talk with some Scottish-Canadian stonemasons on a building site, in front of an adoring crowd, and plunged into the middle of 10,000

The King and Queen visit President and Mrs Roosevelt at Hyde Park, New York, during their North American tour. The Queen is seen chatting to the President's mother.

veterans from the First World War without a qualm. 'The veterans,' said Tweedsmuir, 'made a perfect bodyguard.'

9 June saw a reigning British King and Queen crossing on to American soil, again for the first time in history. It was an arduous experience. The humid heat was intense and there were far too many journalists around. Some few were out to make trouble, some to make a success; none knew precisely what protocol to follow in this entirely unprecedented situation. Their Majesties' welcome in Washington and New York was no less ecstatic than that offered by the Canadians, though even more unexpected. There was no need to point out that King George VI's direct descent from George III was counterbalanced by Queen Elizabeth's kinship with George Washington (through her Smith ancestors on her father's side). Her sparkling crinolines swept all before them, from the senator who said to the King, 'My, you're a great Queen-picker,' to the Secretary of State's young daughter who gasped that she had seen the Fairy Queen. At the World Fair, the crowd sang 'Land of Hope and Glory'.

President Roosevelt and his wife Eleanor were bent on the royal pair enjoying at least a few informal hours in their home at Hyde Park, New York. The tone of informality had already been set in a letter from Roosevelt to the King: 'If you bring either or both of the children with you they will also be very welcome ...'. Despite the absence of 'the children', Roosevelt's hospitality provided the American press with a delightful record of royal naturalness, humanity and democratic tastes. Much was made of hot-dogs eaten at a Hyde Park picnic. Roosevelt mixed his own Manhattans, and as he talked the whole time while doing so, his cocktails were not always as delicious as the hot-dogs. Nevertheless, the affection between the two couples was mutual – and

deeply significant for both their countries. 'They have a way of making friends, these young people,' wrote Mrs Roosevelt. When the war came a bridge had already been thrown across the Atlantic which many others were able to use.

The King and Queen returned home buoyed up by a sense of a strenuous job well done. 'I really believe they like me for myself,' the King's father had said humbly after the triumph of his Silver Jubilee. King George VI came back from his transatlantic tour with the same feeling. Both King and Queen were to say: 'This has made us.'

A month later two very young people enjoyed an experience that was to have a similarly profound effect, and indeed 'make' the future royal dynasty. Princess Elizabeth met and talked to Cadet Captain Philip Mountbatten for the first time at Dartmouth on 22 July 1939. (They had met twice before, at the wedding of the King's youngest brother the Duke of Kent, in 1934, and at the Coronation.) She and her parents and sister were taking a summer break on the royal yacht, *Victoria & Albert*. Through Queen Victoria and Prince Albert the pair were fourth cousins.

Another few weeks passed and on 3 September 1939 the King wrote in his diary: 'Today we are at War again, & I am no longer a midshipman in the Royal Navy' – as he had been on 4 August 1914, keeping the middle watch at midnight on the bridge of HMS *Collingwood*. Nor was the Queen a fourteen-year-old girl bemusedly trying to celebrate her birthday while the crowds around her shouted for war. Today she was the first lady in the land. Would it be a land of defeatism, or could the first lady, together with others of her kind, inspire it to become a 'Land of Hope and Glory'?

The Royal Family visiting Dartmouth with Lord Mountbatten in July 1939. During the visit, Cadet Captain Philip Mountbatten was detailed to entertain Princess Elizabeth and her sister. (He is standing in the middle of the back row, next door to Lord Mountbatten, wearing a white cap.)

The King and Queen at War

5

AT THE BEGINNING of her reign, as we have seen, Queen Elizabeth described kingship as an 'intolerable honour'. Once war had broken out, kingship, and queenship too, were always an intolerable strain and often an intolerable risk. But, as a result of self-imposed duties, the honour in which these Sovereigns were held was doubled and redoubled year by year. 'We have only tried to do our duty during these 5½ years,' the King was to write in his diary after the nation's thanks on VE day. But 'duty' was elastic. People worked out their own idea of it. On some, like the King and Queen, it bore heavily.

The first eight months of the war were 'phoney' or, as the Americans christened it from across the Atlantic, a 'sitzkrieg' rather than the 'blitzkrieg' Hitler had promised. This period was especially frustrating for King George, and therefore for Queen Elizabeth too. He longed in vain for active service, or even for an opportunity to make personal appeals to foreign leaders by letter, or better still to make useful sorties

OPPOSITE *An early colour photograph of the Royal Family at home.*

BELOW *The Queen typically composed before broadcasting to the women of the Empire during the early days of World War II. 'The King and I know what it means to be parted from our children.'*

abroad. He was indeed allowed by his Government to visit the Maginot Line; an ironic treat since it was so soon to be over-run. In April 1940 he was writing, 'Everybody working at fever heat except me.'

What the Government mainly demanded of him was what he hated most: the 'ordeal' of broadcasting to the nation. Year by year his Christmas radio greeting to his people at war, spoken in a fine rich voice, raised their spirits but lowered his appetite to zero. He could never enjoy his Christmas dinner even at that beloved place, Sandringham.

Queen Elizabeth, on the contrary, discovered in herself a remarkable talent for broadcasting. Her voice was as attractive as the King's in its lighter way, and seemed to ripple with pleasure as she spoke, as if a lady dancing a dignified saraband were now and then to give a little skip. A broadcast in French to the women of France was partly drafted for her by the graceful anglophile writer, André Maurois. He had once written a book called *Ariel or The Life of Shelley*. Now he had met 'Titania or The Queen of England'. She told him she did not want an official speech. 'I want a human speech.' The red roses on her table and her sympathetic face already seemed to Maurois impossibly human. His country was invaded, his wife in occupied Paris and he was 'miserable to the point of tears'. Yet here he was, talking to the Queen of England.

Apart from his broadcasts, the King had political work to do, some of it delicate. One problem was the Windsors. Lord Louis Mountbatten had brought Edward to England in his ship HMS *Kelly*, for a brief visit to Windsor Castle. King George noted that his brother looked very well and was quite unworried by the Abdication. 'He has forgotten all about it.' What King George meant was that his brother had forgotten all about the misery he had caused members of his family, who before had been blissfully happy. The Royal Family had not forgotten. When Chamberlain's Government offered Edward the choice of a war job in Wales or Paris, the King chose for him the British Military Mission in Paris. At France's fall the Windsors' fortunes plunged also. Rather than take Wallis to England without a royal title, the Duke escaped with her to Spain, Portugal and finally the Bahamas, where he was appointed Governor for the duration. His adviser and agent, Walter Monckton, became a valued member of the home Government. He was replaced in Edward's counsels, though mostly from afar, by Philip Guedalla, a romantic historian and 'King's man'. The Duke of Windsor had the gift of focusing people's romantic feelings.

Guedalla's biographer, Michael Bloch, tells us that he tried to get Edward a more significant post in South America but failed. Without believing all the tales of plot and counterplot, whether between the Germans and the Windsors to take over in Britain after a Hitler victory, or Guedalla's attempt to get the Windsors home (though not of course on to the throne) – any historian of this period must be aware of the anger and bitterness that poor King George had to face amid all his other troubles, some of it in his own heart. Edward came back to Paris in 1944, after the liberation, with much the same feelings as Napoleon when he was consigned to St Helena. 'Never speak to me again of British fair

Appointed Governor of the Bahamas for the duration of the war, the Duke of Windsor is seen with the Duchess at a Red Cross rally at Government House.

play!' exclaimed the Duke. Elsewhere the Windsors' state of mind has been called galloping paranoia.

The fall of France, meanwhile, had been accompanied by seismic changes in Britain, all of which had sharp repercussions in the Royal Family. The 'miracle' of Dunkirk roused the Queen to heights of patriotic ardour. The heroic salvaging of the Allied armies from the Dunkirk beaches did not seem a 'miracle' at all to Queen Elizabeth. It was just how she would expect the Royal Navy and its swarming civilian supporters in their little ships to behave. When one of her ladies-in-waiting reported 'panic' on the beaches, the Queen stoutly replied, 'I don't believe it. Never say that of the great British people.' It was magnificent; but it was not true of war, where panic and heroism can exist side by side and often do.

Nevertheless the country's mood was predominantly heroic, and a change of Government was demanded in which old-time 'appeasers' would be replaced by all-out war-makers. Mr Chamberlain, sick and deeply tainted with 'appeasement', resigned as Prime Minister, and Lord Halifax, another 'appeaser', wisely refused to offer himself in Chamberlain's place. This left the field open for Winston Churchill. He entered on his historic duties without the spontaneous blessing of the Palace, for King George would have preferred either of the other two. Within a few weeks, however, Churchill's 'lion's roar' (as he was modestly to call his own contribution) found an echo in royal hearts. Moreover, once Churchill's connection with the Abdication, as a 'King's man', had been forgiven, he became far more intimate with the King and

Queen than did any other Minister of their reign. In his diary the King always used the surnames 'Chamberlain' and 'Halifax', whereas Churchill was 'Winston', even at the unpropitious start.

The King's rapport with Churchill had an influence also on the part played by the Queen in the war. Churchill was soon being invited to self-service lunches at the Palace, where he and his Sovereign could continue to confer without being overheard. Queen Elizabeth was often present. And when the air-raids on London began, she would naturally enter the royal air-raid shelter with whatever minister or commander her husband happened to have with him at the moment. Harry Hopkins, President Roosevelt's personal representative, was thus present in 1941. He left an appreciative account of taking cover with the Queen of England:

> The Queen told me that she found it extremely difficult to find words to express her feeling towards the people of Britain in these days. She thought their actions were magnificent and that victory in the long run was sure, but that the one thing that counted was the morale and determination of the great mass of the British people.

ABOVE *Both King and Queen enjoyed a close friendship with Prime Minister Winston Churchill, seen here at 10 Downing Street with Their Majesties.*

RIGHT *Queen Elizabeth joins her daughters Elizabeth and Margaret as they study in a private garden at Windsor Castle.*

Among other delicate subjects, they discussed the future of King Leopold III of the Belgians.

The first point to notice in regard to the Queen's inner knowledge of events is her absolute discretion. No one will ever know quite how much she heard, for she never told anyone. From the very beginning of the war her Household noticed her reserve: 'She seldom said anything about what she was thinking.' The truth was that this outgoing responsive Queen knew also how to keep her own counsel. There was a vein of strength in her character that friends did not always suspect. The Abdication, for instance, she has virtually never mentioned to the vast majority of her friends. She has mentioned it to a very few others, but only since the death of the Duke of Windsor.

When the European sitzkrieg became a blitzkrieg in the spring and summer of 1940, there was a move to get the Royal Family away, perhaps into the safekeeping of Canada. The Dominions were already giving hospitality to hundreds of British children. Far from belittling their generosity, the Queen was to send a special letter of thanks to all the people of the Dominions who had offered homes in the hour of need. But for herself and her family? The voice of duty told her that this was not for her or hers. She said more than once: 'The children could not go without me, I could not possibly leave the King, and the King would never go.' To Harold Nicolson, who spoke to her of being homesick for his castle and garden in Kent, she said of her own castle at Windsor, 'I should die if I had to leave.'

She was none the less separated from her children all day anyway, and sometimes for days on end. The two Princesses spent most of their war behind the huge stone fortifications of Windsor Castle, or beneath them, during an alert. Down they would troop with their parents to the shelters under a medieval tower, the Princesses equipped with two small suitcases

presented to them by the French after their parents' Paris visit in 1938. The cases had been part of two dolls' outfits, but now held their owners' most precious treasures.

The 'Fort' which they had hitherto connected with Windsor was Uncle David's Fort Belvedere. Now their own home was fortified and they themselves guarded by twelve young officers from the Brigade of Guards. Life would have been dull for the Princesses without them. Their parents started for London every morning at eight o'clock, come wind, come weather or come air-raid warning. Elizabeth and Margaret were left with their governesses, Miss Crawford and Mrs Smith, until the King and Queen returned just in time for dinner.

One of the officers remembers the Long Corridor, utterly blank for lack of pictures, which were in store, and with its remaining furniture pushed back to the wall. Sir Gerald Kelly was still painting the official pictures of the Coronation, including what Lady Buxton called 'two small and *ghaastly* [sic] portraits' of the Queen. This young Guardsman returned to Windsor Castle for a second spell of duty in the spring of 1941. Now it was the Queen's magic which he remembered.

One evening she returned late from London after a *dreadful* day. Hundreds of houses down, streets up, people crying. The lot. But she came down to the

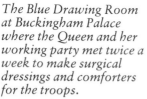

The Blue Drawing Room at Buckingham Palace where the Queen and her working party met twice a week to make surgical dressings and comforters for the troops.

Her Majesty greets an East-Ender in Stepney during one of the many visits the Sovereigns made in London.

Quadrangle to see us at the Household dinner in the Star Chamber, as she always did, and laughed and joked with the children. And *what* she was like with the King! For ever loving and soothing ...

As Europe was over-run, Queen Elizabeth found her hands full with other royal persons needing her love and care. She looked after Princess Victoria, 1st Marchioness of Milford Haven and Lord Mountbatten's mother, at Windsor Castle for the rest of the war. The Queen's daughters were strictly enjoined to take this remarkable old lady for a walk every day. Lilibet and Margaret reported easy progress down the Castle hill but difficulties in getting the princess up again.

Homes had to be found for Queen Wilhelmina of the Netherlands (who brought only the clothes she stood up in plus a tin hat), her daughter Princess Juliana and two small granddaughters, Beatrix and Irene, the latter a baby whom Queen Elizabeth arranged to have christened in the chapel of Buckingham Palace. It was the last royal christening before the chapel received its own baptism of fire from a flying-bomb.

King Haakon of Norway was another royal refugee; and though General de Gaulle was not royal he was as hard to please as if he had been the great mogul himself. Churchill called de Gaulle his 'cross of Lorraine' and was not sorry to see the last of him in 1944. But when he left, de Gaulle said to the King and Queen: 'You are the only two people who have always shown me humanity and understanding.' It was a well-earned tribute to the part of conciliators played by Their Majesties in war.

The problems of less exalted exiles were also close to the Queen's heart. Burdened by the hideous bureaucratic name of 'evacuees',

After a London hospital had become a casualty of Nazi bombings, their Majesties visited to talk with the patients, such as this injured fireman.

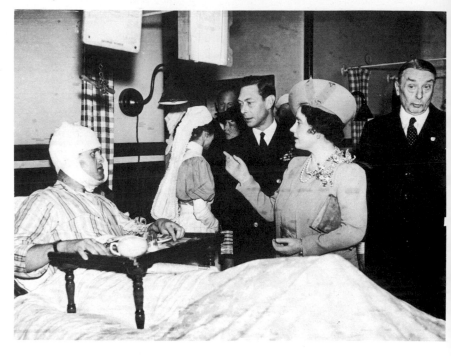

thousands of mothers and children, as well as unaccompanied children, were received by country hosts whose way of life they did not understand or like. At first there was great chaos. Five hundred lost gas-masks were collected from a single 'evacuee' train at Paddington station. The unhappy evacuees were always balancing up the possibility of sudden death at home against the certainty of living death in exile. They were liable to decamp without a kind word, leaving behind hosts who were as thankful to get rid of them as they were ruffled at the mode of their going. It fell to the Queen to speak the grateful word that poor harried human nature had no time for. Thousands of letters of thanks were sent all over the country on Palace writing-paper to those who had welcomed official evacuees.

Travelling from city to city in the royal train there were occasions when Queen Elizabeth did not see her daughters even at night. This way of life was something of an innovation. In the days of King George v the Royal couple would stay with the *haute noblesse* when opening a hospital or launching a ship. King George vi was too shy to enjoy this kind of visiting, even when a Lord-Lieutenant of a county was available to entertain them; he preferred his own small circle of friends. During the war no accommodation was available, except the royal train. Here indeed the King was comfortable and at ease, alone with a tiny staff and his all-important wife. The train was equipped as a mobile home, down to telephonic connection with the Palace. From this base they would visit hospitals, barracks, ARP centres, Home Guard stations, balloon barrages and the hundred other outward signs of a country at war.

The Battle of Britain had begun. London was savagely raided with fire-bombs for the first time on 7 September. The operation was intended by Hitler to soften up his island foe in preparation for its invasion by sea and air. The royal timetable, already dutifully full, suddenly acquired a quite new urgency as King George and Queen Elizabeth visited the bombed sites, breathing in dust and giving what sympathy and help they could. The Queen's cousin, Lilian Bowes-Lyon, was working devotedly in the East End. In response to her appeal, the Queen collected piles of unused Victorian furniture from the royal attics and stores to help replenish the homes that Hitler had destroyed.

That January of 1941 she visited Sheffield, a blitzed city. Lord Harlech, the Midlands Commissioner, told Harold Nicolson how, when her car stopped, 'the Queen nips out into the snow and goes straight into the middle of the crowd and starts talking to them. First they would just gape; then they all started talking at once – "Hi! Your Majesty! Look here!"'

The Queen had to think more carefully than ever about how to appear among the stricken families. As soon as war broke out she had made one firm decision. 'Some clothes do not like me,' she would say, and among these were uniforms. She never wore them. Similarly, her light girlish fringe had vanished three years before; she had decided it was one of the things that 'did not like her' as Queen. Hitherto her usual choice of

King George VI and Queen Elizabeth; tireless in their efforts among their people.

*An American admirer's
tribute to Britain's Queen.*

colours, carried out by Hartnell, had been for rainbow hues. But as Wordsworth said, 'The rainbow comes and goes' – and now it had to go. Hartnell collected a series of 'dusty' shades, especially blues, lilacs and what used to be called 'dirty pink', which would neither strike the poor people as too light-hearted, nor show too much of the actual dust from bomb sites. Nevertheless, the Queen always made an effort to wear her best when visiting the people. 'Of course I do,' she said. 'If the poor people came to see me they would put on their best clothes.'

Though not superstitious herself, the Queen banished both black and green from her wardrobe, as liable to seem 'unlucky' to those who had already been hit by enough bad luck to last them a lifetime. In her 'dusty' coloured clothes she was thus admirably equipped to render even the oddest kind of first aid. 'I am rather good with dogs,' she said one day as she offered to coax a trembling terrier out of a dust-hole where it had been buried. The Queen's voice brought it once more into the light of day. 'Oh, ain't she luverley,' said someone, perhaps in that very crowd round the dog, 'ain't she just bloody luverley'; it was certainly in the accents of the post-war musical, *My Fair Lady.*

Queen Elizabeth's greatest triumph with Hartnell was to persuade the famous couturier to design 'utility' clothes for ordinary people. With the strict rationing of clothes, as of everything else, it seemed sensible that the dresses available should at least be well designed. Hartnell hesitated at first. Dare he, the master of silver tissue and cloth of gold, put his name to positively banal materials? But he would do anything for the Queen.

Now came the most dramatic moment of the Queen's 'war'. It was due to the daring and accuracy of a German bomber-pilot, who suddenly decided to fly straight up the Mall, beneath the cloud-cover, and drop a stick of six bombs across the heartland of his British enemies. The date was 12 September 1940. After it was all over a Palace policeman said to the Queen, 'A magnificent piece of bombing, Ma'am, if you'll pardon my saying so.' It was the first bombing of Buckingham Palace.

Their Majesties' very narrow escape was kept a deadly secret even from the Prime Minister and Government. It was part of censorship madness. Though the bombing of the Palace could not be concealed, Their Majesties' heroic endurance *could* be concealed, and was. Yet knowledge of what they had been through could have done nothing but good.

The King's account of the bombing is poignant in its spareness:

All of a sudden we heard an aircraft making a zooming noise above us, saw 2 bombs falling past the opposite side of the Palace, & then heard 2 resounding crashes as the bombs fell in the quadrangle about 30 yards away. We looked at each other & then we were out into the passage as fast as we could get there. . . . We all wondered why we weren't dead. . . . It was a ghastly experience, & I don't want it to be repeated. It certainly teaches one to 'take cover' on all future occasions, but one must be careful not to become 'dugout minded'.

At first they used as a 'dugout' a small basement room, where the burly presence of an outsize housemaid seemed somehow reassuring.

Soon, however, a fully equipped concrete shelter was built alongside the Palace.

For a week after 12 September the King found himself unable to read and for ever glancing out of the window. Rats moved in from broken sewers, and the King and Queen moved out – but only for the nights, which they spent at Windsor.

With her more buoyant temperament, the Queen probably suffered a less severe shock than the King. Indeed, to be public figures and to be bombed, she realized, had its compensations. It emphasized their humanity. Death in a palace is no different from death in a tenement. 'I am glad we have been bombed,' said the Queen; 'I feel I can look the East End in the face.'

The novelist Rose Macaulay had written ironically to her sister six days before the Buckingham Palace bombing that they must all be 'grim and gay about the raids, as Churchill says. I suppose gay when oneself and one's friends aren't hit, but grim when they are.' Queen Elizabeth

'A magnificent piece of bombing, Ma'am, if you'll pardon my saying so,' reported a policeman to the Queen after Buckingham Palace had received a direct hit in 1940.

The Queen is joined by Princess Elizabeth on yet another wartime royal visit.

had reversed the joke and felt almost gay to think that it was 'oneself'.

Nor would she be caught by possible German parachutists without a fight. While King George was being trained to use a tommy-gun on home ranges at Windsor and Buckingham Palace, Queen Elizabeth was adding to her skills by learning to fire a revolver. Harold Nicolson expressed amazement. 'Yes,' she said to him resolutely, 'I shall not go down like the others.'

The King cherished a secret determination to lead a British 'Resistance Movement', if it ever came to that. And no doubt his wife would have taken the role of a tiny but irrepressible Queen Boadicea.

One day King Haakon asked King George to demonstrate an anti-parachute alert in the Palace garden. King George pressed a button and – nothing happened. The outside warning to the lodge had not been received, and so with British phlegm the lodge-keeper told those who should have reported at action stations to take no notice of the alarm.

Meanwhile the range of Buckingham Palace was alive with pops and bangs. Lord Halifax, who had been given permission to use the Palace garden as a short cut to his office, was puzzled the first time he heard the shots and enquired their cause. 'Her Majesty's target practice,' was the reply. As his path ran nearby, he decided it might prove a short cut to the next world and chose another route to work.

German parachutists were not the only potential invaders whom Queen Elizabeth had to fend off. One day a half-crazed deserter whose family had all been killed in a raid found his way into the Queen's bedroom, threw himself at her feet and seized her by the ankles. It was like some scene from the Middle Ages. 'For a moment my heart stood absolutely still,' remembered the Queen. Then, 'Tell me about it,' she said quietly, realizing that if she screamed he might attack her. He poured out his sad tale as she moved step by step towards the bell. 'Poor man, I was so sorry for him,' she said afterwards.

Hitler's invasion of Russia in June 1941 and the Japanese attack on Pearl Harbor in the following December brought Russia and America into the war. The friendship between Their Majesties and President Roosevelt, struck up at Hyde Park in 1939, had not been allowed to rust during the two years of American neutrality. In all his many letters to 'My Dear President Roosevelt', King George would include the name of Queen Elizabeth: 'The Queen & I', 'The Queen joins me in ...', 'The Queen ...'

Four months before Pearl Harbor the Queen herself had broadcast to the women of America. Roosevelt described it as 'really perfect in every way'. Early in March 1942 the family connection was further emphasized by her brother David Bowes-Lyon carrying a letter across the Atlantic from King to President.

The first check to Hitler's armies took place in the Western desert, in July 1942. A month later, on 25 August, tragedy struck the Royal Family. While at Balmoral the King heard that his youngest brother George of Kent, a favourite with everyone, had been killed when his RAF plane crashed into a mountain at Morven, on a flight to Iceland. 'This news came as a great shock to me, & I had to break it to Elizabeth ...' wrote the King. 'He was killed on Active Service.' The two capital letters showed how large 'Active Service' loomed in the King's order of priorities. Grief gave a fillip to his own frustration, which was never far below the surface.

For the time being, however, his mind was occupied by a visit from Eleanor Roosevelt, the President's wife, to Buckingham Palace. A letter from the President explained her mission in the tone of a friend and equal:

I want you and the Queen to tell Eleanor everything in regard to problems of our troops in England which she might not get from the Government or military authorities.

There was only one sign of a difference in status. While Roosevelt referred to his wife as 'Eleanor', King George always referred to his as 'the Queen'. Roosevelt added:

You and I know that it is the little things which count but which are not always set forth in official reports.

The 'little things' disclosed by that shrewd observer, Eleanor Roosevelt, about wartime life in Buckingham Palace would no doubt have shocked officialdom. They fascinate posterity, proving as they do that the royal pair were not enjoying luxuries denied to their subjects.

The Queen gave up her bedroom to her honoured American guest. A formidably spacious apartment, it was heated inadequately for the time of year (late October) with a one-bar electric fire. Perhaps it was

fortunate that the large plate-glass windows had all been blown out by one or other of the nine bombings to which the Palace had by then been subjected. Small wooden frames had been knocked up inside the gaping casements, 'glazed' with mica. One smallish sitting-room was warm, being heated with a coal fire. Otherwise, 'Buckingham Palace is an enormous place,' wrote Mrs Roosevelt, 'and without heat.' Both the King and Queen had colds.

Fuel was of course rationed, and the Palace abided by its scanty quota of electricity. This affected hot baths also. A 'Plimsoll line' was painted five inches from the bottom of every bath. Among the pleasures of victory would be soaking in a deep bath once again.

The same austerity affected the Palace food. Tasteless wartime food (because no butter and hardly any other fats found their way into the cooking) was borne into the dining-room on silver and gold dishes. Wartime delicacies included dehydrated reconstituted eggs, and pies, puddings and jams made of root vegetables. The Queen would blithely dismiss them as 'probably sawdust'. But as to whether it was Woolton Pie (called after the Food Minister) or a birthday cake produced for Mrs Roosevelt that first earned this royal compliment, writers are not agreed.

By June 1943 the King's longing for active service was satisfied to some extent by a flying visit to his victorious troops in North Africa. Now it was the Queen's turn to suffer as she waited at the Palace for news. The King's visit was literally a 'flying' one, and who could tell what fog and enemy action between them might achieve? No doubt the Duke of Kent's tragic accident added to her fears.

I have had an anxious few hours [she wrote to Queen Mary] because at 8.15 I heard that the plane had been heard near Gibraltar, and that it would soon be landing. Then after an hour & a half I heard that there was a thick fog at Gib. & that they were going on to Africa. Then complete silence till a few minutes ago, when a message came that they have landed in Africa, & taken off again. Of course I imagined every sort of horror, & walked up and down my room staring at the telephone.

Equally profound feelings, but of a wholly satisfying kind, flooded the King and Queen when Princess Elizabeth celebrated her eighteenth birthday at Windsor on 21 April 1944. There was a family luncheon composed, one hopes, not entirely of 'sawdust'. At the King's wish, Princess Elizabeth was created a Counsellor of State; at her own wish she plunged the next year into war service, becoming in time a junior transport officer of the Auxiliary Territorial Service. Her subsequent delight in the anatomy of heavy lorries drew from her mother the comment, 'We had sparking plugs all last night at dinner.' The Queen herself at eighteen had travelled behind an old horse who fell asleep in the middle of the road.

D-Day arrived less than two months after the Princess's birthday, on 6 June 1944. King George and Queen Elizabeth spent the day waiting and wondering together in a torment of anxiety. Knowing her husband, the

King George with Princess Elizabeth who, at her own wish, had been allowed to become a junior transport officer with the Auxiliary Territorial Service, the ATS.

Queen had wanted him to fulfil his passion for active service by accompanying the assault force as it made for the Normandy beaches. It had been Churchill's original idea to do so, and the King at once decided to jump on Churchill's bandwagon – or rather, aboard his battleship. 'I told Elizabeth about the idea,' wrote the King in his diary on 30 May, '& she was wonderful as always & encourged me to do it.' However, Sir Alan Lascelles, now the King's Private Secretary, was appalled at the double risk and persuaded his master to forgo his own pleasure and veto Churchill's also. In the event no harm came to any of the ships which might have carried the august complement.

In July, however, the King was flown to Europe for ten days' inspection of his armies in Italy. 'He feels so much not being more in the fighting line,' wrote his wife to his mother. The two women well understood the King's conflicts. He would always profoundly prefer action to kingship, but it was not his to choose.

Meanwhile, Queen Elizabeth was thinking ruefully about the last stages of Hitlerite aggression: the flying bombs and rockets. As usual she unburdened herself to Queen Mary. 'There is something very inhuman about death-dealing missiles being launched in such an indiscriminate manner,' she wrote. One 'doodle-bug' had seemed mindlessly to pursue her two daughters for a few hectic minutes, before exploding on the Windsor racecourse.

Incidentally the Queen's many letters to her mother-in-law were one entirely happy result of Queen Mary's lonely war. She was evacuated to Badminton in the West Country for the duration. Without that long separation, many of Queen Elizabeth's piquant sayings would have been lost to history.

Victory in Europe came on 8 May 1945, and it came to the Royal Family assembled on the famous balcony of Buckingham Palace. They were called back again and again, taking all together eight 'curtain calls'. The balcony itself, it transpired, was by no means as safe as houses – or only as safe as bombed houses, having been badly shaken by successive blasts. The historic photograph shows, behind the royal group, a small boarded-up casement, rather than the tall windows recently made familiar again by Princess Anne's wedding photograph.

The Queen is wearing exactly the same hat and coat that she was to

VE Day. The King and Queen on the balcony of Buckingham Palace together with the Prime Minister Winston Churchill, Princess Elizabeth and Princess Margaret.

*'Sketch' for the portrait
by Sir Gerald Kelly of HM
Queen Elizabeth
painted during the war
years.*

wear again on other joyful occasions, for pretty clothes still had to do
duty many times. There are two uniforms on the balcony: the King's and
Princess Elizabeth's. In the centre of the group stands Winston Churchill,
grinning modestly, hands in pockets. On his left is King George with a
half smile, holding up his hand perhaps a little wearily. On Churchill's
right is Queen Elizabeth, her wave the gayest, her smile the one to
remember.

Peace and the Family 6

'THIS HAS MADE US,' said the King and Queen after their visit to the New World. Six years later they might have said even more emphatically, 'This war has made us.' The shared experience had indeed set its seal on their popularity, their total credibility. It had also left its mark on both of them as people.

The King was to describe himself as 'burnt out'. The Queen had sometimes felt emotionally drained even before the war was over. 'I feel quite exhausted after seeing and hearing so much sadness, sorrow, heroism and magnificent spirit,' she wrote to Queen Mary as early as 1940. 'The destruction is so awful and the people are so *wonderful* – they *deserve* a better world.'

A better world. The King and Queen ardently hoped to preserve the country's unity through a continuation of the coalition that had won the war. It was not to be. A democracy must give the people a choice of government. In Britain there had been no General Election – no freedom of choice – for ten years, in fact not since 1935 when King George V was still on the throne.

Those days of social division and bitterness seemed worlds away and must not be allowed to return. Even during the worst moments of the war, the suffering had been shared. The pent-up longing for 'a better world' was focused by 1945 upon the idea of a Welfare State. When it burst out at last, the Labour Party was swept to power in a landslide victory.

Queen Elizabeth was far too discreet to allow her personal reactions any expression. She was a romantic, however, with a delight in history. She responded to light, colour and elegance, whether in the present or the past. But there was not much colour and a good deal of brashness in the post-war present. Austerities were conscientiously and perhaps unnecessarily prolonged by the Labour Government, in the interests of 'fair shares for all'. The King felt bound to tackle Clement Attlee, his new Prime Minister, on behalf of his wife and daughters. 'I said we must have new clothes & my family are down to the lowest ebb.'

The Labour Government at first made an unfavourable impression on the King, despite his being, in the words of his official biographer, 'a progressive in political thought and a reformer in social conscience'. King George told his brother Henry, Duke of Gloucester, that the Government 'is not too easy & the people are rather difficult to talk to'. This last point applied particularly to the Prime Minister. Attlee was as shy and silent as

OPPOSITE *July 1947: 'It is with the greatest pleasure that the King and Queen announce the betrothal of their beloved daughter . . .' Princess Elizabeth with her fiancé, her parents and sister.*

the King himself. Silent types were not to the King's taste. During the war
he had regretfully described Mr and Mrs George Winant, the American
ambassador and his wife, as 'silent people'. Mr James Byrnes, on the
contrary, the American Secretary of State, was not at all silent. 'At lunch I
talked to Mr Byrnes,' the King wrote. 'I liked him. Attractive of Irish
origin and a great talker.'

The silences of the King and of Major Attlee were very different in
origin, as Attlee recognized when he wrote sympathetically of the King:
'He is rather the worrying type ... I'm not a worrier.'

A large part of the King's gloom was due to the loss of Winston
Churchill as Prime Minister. A man of intense loyalty, King George in
1945 regretted Churchill's supersession by Attlee as much as in 1940 he
had deplored Chamberlain's replacement by Churchill.

The main cause of the King's immediate post-war depression was due
to his physical and mental exhaustion. One has only to compare
photographs of the royal couple making their public appearances at the
beginning and end of the war to see the difference. By the end, the King's
face was thin and his jawline sharp. This was far from so during the early
1940s. At Lichfield there is a particular photograph of the King and
Queen on the steps of the Guildhall, he wearing RAF uniform. His
features still give the impression of youthful contours, reminding one of
the young Prince of Wales his brother. The Queen's hat has flowers in it.
They exemplified what Harold Nicolson meant when he wrote to his
wife about Their Majesties in 1940:

The Royal Family in
Windsor Great Park.

I cannot tell you how superb she was. I anticipated her charm. What astonished me is how the King has changed. He is now like his brother. He was so gay and she so calm.

The contrast appears in a scene described, again by Harold Nicolson, on 17 May 1945. This was a parliamentary ceremony performed by Their Majesties in the Royal Gallery of the House of Lords. First the King made a long speech, wrote Nicolson, in his 'really beautiful voice'. He was listened to in silence, for the strains of the last years had brought back his tendency to hesitations and long pauses. Nicolson considered the silence 'ungrateful' in view of the excellent work that the King had done. Fortunately on this occasion Winston Churchill was still 'caretaker' Premier. He broke the silence by calling for three cheers. 'All our pent up energies responded with three yells,' wrote Nicolson, 'such as I should have thought impossible to emanate from so many elderly throats.'

Those elderly male cheers were surely directed also at Queen Elizabeth, for Nicolson's diary gives due weight to her remarkable presence:

Then they walked down the aisle which separated the Lords from the Commons; very slowly they walked, bowing to right and left. The Queen has a truly miraculous faculty of making each individual feel that it is him whom she has greeted and to him that was devoted that lovely smile. She has a true genius for her job.

What Nicolson apparently did not realize was that King George and none other had helped Queen Elizabeth to do 'her job' with such consummate success.

The change had come imperceptibly after the Abdication. When the Yorks were first married a friend said, 'Of course *she* will wear the trousers.' Apart from the impossibility of visualizing Queen Elizabeth in trousers (except years before when on safari) this picture of their relationship was never true. Both as royal duchess and as Queen, Elizabeth held a Christian view of marriage which creates a partnership of genuine equality based on love. Her respect for the mystique of kingship would have rendered any ordinary self-assertiveness unthinkable.

Besides, it was not in her nature to dominate. By the time war broke out their partnership was recognized as touchingly mutual by all who were close to them. Queen Elizabeth's sisters, Lady (Rose) Granville and Lady (Jean) Elphinstone, have each put their finger on the truth, pointing out how greatly the Queen had come to rely on her husband. 'They were so particularly together,' said Lady Elphinstone: 'they both leant so much on the other.' And Lady Granville said, 'The King was a rock to her, indeed to all of us. In fundamental things she leant on him: I have always felt how much the Queen was sustained by the King.'

In this ideal relationship the King and Queen were to spend their remaining six-and-a-half years together: a time of peace and challenge for the nation and of new interests and achievements for themselves. Over and over again their biographers have rightly stressed their original unwillingness to accept sovereignty, and their preference for a more private life. Less has been made of what must be equally true: the pleasure and strength that they derived from regal duties superbly performed.

To have asked them whether they enjoyed their high estate, and wished thus to continue, would have been a meaningless question. Nevertheless, the atmosphere in the Palace between 1937 and 1939 was very different from that between 1945 and 1952. It was the difference between an uncongenial career forced upon them, and a career through which they had come to express their fullest potentialities of service.

A final clue to the Queen's happy and equal partnership with her husband may be extracted from an unexpected quarter. In a successful speech to a school, Queen Elizabeth was to recommend three qualities which seemed to her eminently worthy of cultivation. All three began with the letter D: *discernment* or the power to judge what needs doing, *decision* to act, *designing* a plan of action. These 'three Ds', it will be noted, are the special qualities of men and women of action. They all fit the King's character admirably, and whether consciously or uncon-

King George and Queen Elizabeth at the castle built by Queen Victoria and Prince Albert – Balmoral.

sciously, it was for these fine qualities among others that the Queen so greatly relied on him.

Decisiveness especially was a quality that the Queen saw exemplified in her husband, and for which she relied on him to complement her own more relaxed though strong character and great talent for empathy.

The complementary nature of their relationship was again seen in the revived hobbies and pleasures of peacetime. In gardening, for instance, the King was interested in the lay-out and 'bones' of a garden, while the Queen looked for the soft haze of colour and scent. All the Wales boys had inherited a love of gardening from their mother, Queen Mary. (The Rose Garden in the Botanical Gardens of Regent's Park was named after her.) In the old days observers on both sides of the royal fence had described with astonishment the furious labours of David in slashing and pruning the jungle of Fort Belvedere and the equal determination of Bertie in clearing and redesigning the landscape of Royal Lodge. Now the delights of gardening were resumed wherever possible by George VI in England, while the Duke of Windsor was pushing his wheelbarrow in France. But whereas the Duchess of Windsor could never resist the additional smartness of expensive cut flowers from the shops to decorate her immaculate house, the Queen of England loved to grow in her own gardens all the flowers for her homes.

The grander the banquet the greater the challenge to the royal gardeners, rather than to the florists. A team of lady-gardeners would bring armfuls of flowers into the Waterloo Chamber at Windsor. Strips of felt would be laid on the long polished table, on either side of huge silver *épergnes* which were to receive the flower arrangements. Up would climb the ladies on to the table, and soon there would be a row of shining bowls filled with the scented beauty of roses, lilies and sweet peas. Meanwhile the King would concentrate on the 'ideas' department of the royal 'firm', thinking out new schemes for landscaping and design.

At Balmoral or Sandringham the 'division of labour' between King and Queen was just as evident. The King was a brilliant shot, though temperamentally perhaps too quick off the mark for perfection. Queen Elizabeth's expertise with the rod was of the same star quality. Her chief delight was not in the formal and meticulously organized occasions when the ladies would join the guns for luncheon, but in relaxed and carefree picnics on the Scottish moors. She particularly loved a little unused school house above Balmoral. Here the Queen would put a match to the wood fire and unpack the picnic basket. Afterwards her daughters would run down to the burn to wash up the plates and cups, while their mother fished in a favourite pool.

Lady Airlie noticed that the atmosphere of Sandringham was more homely than it had ever been before – and she had known it under four different regimes. In the King's mind it all pivoted on the Queen. 'You must ask Mummy,' he would say when his daughters came to him with requests; and when Lady Airlie praised the script of his 1945 Christmas broadcast, he looked across at his wife and said, 'She helped me.' In the Queen's mind life revolved around the King.

8 June 1946. From a dais on the Mall, King and Queen, princes, princesses and statesmen salute the armed forces.

There were many official and State celebrations to be undertaken in those first post-war·years. The first State dinner at Buckingham Palace was given in honour of Queen Wilhelmina of the Netherlands. A thorough mixture of guests was present, indicative of an old world changing into a new. A member of the old aristocracy could not bring himself to bow to Edwina Mountbatten, as she left with the rest of the royal party. Despite her arduous and dedicated war-work, she was not 'royal'. Nevertheless, the Royal Family attended the weddings of both her daughters, Patricia and Pamela. (Princess Elizabeth and Princess Margaret were bridesmaids to Patricia.) On the other hand, an Old Etonian member of the new Labour Government brought a wife whose clothing coupons did not run to a pair of long white gloves. It seemed to many guests that the old and the new were epitomized in the welcomes given to them by Queen Mary and Queen Elizabeth respectively. The old Queen sat beautifully upright and immobile, while her lady-in-waiting brought up one Labour lady after another in quick succession, to make polite conversation. Scarcely a minute would pass before Queen Mary was signalling, 'Next, please', to her lady-in-waiting, the signal not infrequently being intercepted by the unsuccessful conversationalist, who then realized that she had failed to amuse.

How different to be led up to Queen Elizabeth! Always graceful and relaxed, with eyes that danced and head that turned slightly this way and that as she spoke, to make a point or ask a question, Queen Elizabeth seemed to have all the time in the world and every intention of prolonging the pleasure of her current conversation. As often as not she would end a sentence with, 'Don't you think so?' or 'Isn't it?' thereby inviting a sense of agreement and shared experience. The King once said of her, 'Elizabeth can make a home anywhere.' He might have added that she could make anyone *feel at home* anywhere, even in Buckingham Palace.

The first post-war garden party at Buckingham Palace was given for those who had slaved throughout the war on behalf of the movement for National Savings. So great was the excitement of the guests that at one point Their Majesties looked like being totally submerged by thousands of enthusiasts, to the understandable anxiety of the Household. The King and Queen, however, afterwards expressed their pleasure at having been so loyally mobbed.

Even greater crowds were able to see their Sovereigns at the Victory Parade on 8 June 1946. The march-past took place in the Mall, where a saluting platform had been erected. Behind Their Majesties and on each side of them sat the leaders of Parliament and the Services; below them on two chairs Winston Churchill and Clement Attlee, one in a top hat, the other bareheaded. On the platform stood the King and Queen side by side, burning with patriotic pride.

1947 was to bring a great joint experience for the Royal Family, perhaps the greatest *family* experience of their lives, in terms of time, energy and mutual support – the visit to South Africa. It was preceded, however, by an event that demanded all the royal pair's loving tact.

A silver wedding photograph of Their Majesties at Buckingham Palace, April 1948.

By 1946 it was abundantly clear to the whole family that Princess Elizabeth and Prince Philip of Greece were in love. Indeed the Princess had been in love since she was seventeen, though her parents were not having any 'child marriages' in their family, as in the days of Queen Victoria's eldest daughter. The King wrote to Queen Mary: 'We both think she is too young for that now', upon which Queen Mary remarked sagely to Lady Airlie: 'After all, he had to wait long enough for *his* wife, and you can see what a success their marriage is.'

Prince Philip had risen to the rank of lieutenant while serving in the British Navy. He had had a brilliant war, with hair's-breadth escapes and decorations to his credit. He was evidently a prospective son-in-law after the King's heart. His character was strong, his appearance handsome as that of a young Viking, his record remarkably distinguished, his brain exceptional, his athletic skill outstanding and his birth royal. Two considerations none the less weighed with the King against an immediate marriage for his beloved elder daughter and heir. Neither she nor Margaret was in the slightest degree worldly-wise. Owing to the war they had met scarcely any men of their own age. Curiously enough, the King did not entertain for them overmuch, even after the war was over. And here we enter the second layer of reasoning and feeling which caused the King to postpone the Princess's engagement.

His family love and loyalty were of an intensity that is perhaps only seen in those who have missed the pleasures of warmth and closeness in their own childhood. Marriage had brought Prince Bertie a shower of warmth, beauty and elegance, both inwardly and in his surroundings. Within a decade his family was a perfect quartet. To remove one member of this team would inevitably spoil it; not only for himself, but for his younger daughter also, who might be left lonely and exposed.

The word 'possessive' has sometimes been used of King George VI. It would be true only of the King in respect to his feelings for the family *as a whole*, not for particular individuals. Those who have called him possessive often go on to say that Queen Elizabeth was not. In so far as possessiveness springs from early deprivation, the Queen's own happy childhood left her with a legacy of confidence which she could pass on to others. She had no instinctive fear of losing her children by their marriages, any more than Lord and Lady Strathmore had lost her through hers. She could afford to be liberal with her family, partly because it was to her an entirely natural unit – something she loved and almost took for granted – whose development she expected and understood. Born to happiness and trust, she gave these great gifts to her husband also, though not all at once. It needed time to dissolve all his inborn fears.

By chance in February 1946 a question arose which amply justified the King in keeping the family four-square and intact for at least another year. The Governor-General of South Africa, Gideon Brand Van Zyl, invited the Royal Family to visit his country early in the following year, when the King would perform the State Opening of Parliament on 27 February 1947. He would be accompanied by Queen Elizabeth and the two Princesses.

To the King this was a most important invitation from the point of view of the Commonwealth. Mr Gideon Brand Van Zyl was the first ever Governor-General of South Africa to have been born there. King George well knew how deeply South Africa was riven by nationalist politics. And not only South Africa. Burma was actually to leave the Empire in 1947, the first country to secede since the United States in 1776. King George had longed to visit India, Burma and South-East Asia during the war, partly to strengthen Imperial ties, partly to encourage his Forgotten Army. 'A visit from me,' he rightly said, 'would buck them up.' He was furious at being thwarted, blaming it afterwards in jest on Winston Churchill's spirit of emulation – 'I've got the Star of Burma and he hasn't.'

The King had also flared up before the war when he learned that he would not be allowed to visit India for a Coronation Durbar. 'It's P.J. Grigg!' he said. Grigg of the India Office had insisted that India could not afford a Durbar. But George VI had simply wanted to make contact with his Indian peoples, rather than pour out money.

1947, besides marking the loss of Burma, was also to be the final year of the British Raj in India. The King's cousins, Lord and Lady Mountbatten, were to be appointed, that same February, the last Viceroy and Vicereine – and, among modern viceregal incumbents, the most successful.

The invitation from South Africa for the Royal Family was accepted on 3 March 1946. The King's various arguments for going in full strength were certainly not contested by the Queen, even though, in other circumstances, she might have agreed to the twenty-year-old Princess Elizabeth's engagement. It was sad for Elizabeth to be parted from Philip for over three long months; but the Queen was profoundly aware of Elizabeth's steadfast character. She was not one to change her mind, however many men she met.

Not surprisingly, Princess Margaret backed up her sister in the arguments for an earlier engagement. According to the King's biographer, the Queen and her husband thrashed out all questions with their children. Nothing was forbidden them or put beyond the pale of discussion. The children had come to think of their parents as almost one single personality rather than two separate people. And so the King, in telling Queen Mary about the postponed engagement, could truthfully say: 'We *both* think she is too young for that now.'

Great preparations were made for this State visit. It was a pleasure, after war shortages and post-war austerity, to have a duty to shine in the sun. The royal party were to travel in HMS *Vanguard*, Britain's newest battleship. No doubt *Vanguard* was to prove as susceptible to the Queen's charm as *Enchantress* had been nine years before. Among other things, the Queen was always on deck and on top form. Never in her life did she suffer from seasickness, or airsickness.

Mr Hartnell was again right on his toes. During the war the Queen's satin dresses could not be embroidered with beads or diamanté, in the interests of economy. Instead, Hartnell had resorted to hand-painted flowers. Now embroidery was back. Ostrich feathers were also prominent in Her Majesty's trousseau – in honour of South Africa's bird rather than with any suggestion of heads in sand. On the Princesses' white yachting jackets Hartnell had sewn brass buttons of an authentic naval design. The King himself always dressed immaculately and was as particular as his father and grandfather about correct attire. Naval buttons on civilian dresses were incorrect, and therefore the King ordered them to be replaced by plain ones.

A high-powered and exceptionally charming group of people was mobilized to attend on Their Majesties, among them Sir Alan ('Tommy') Lascelles as the King's private secretary with Major Michael Adeane (later Queen Elizabeth II's private secretary and a peer) as assistant; Major Tom Harvey, on his first royal tour, as private secretary to the Queen; Lady Harlech and Lady Delia Peel as ladies-in-waiting to the Queen; Lady Margaret ('Meg') Egerton, now Lady Margaret Colville, as lady-in-waiting to the Princesses; Wing-Commander Peter Townsend as an equerry.

The royal party were well aware how incredibly strenuous the tour was going to be. When Princess Elizabeth first saw the printed itinerary she simply said, 'Well, I hope we shall survive, that's all.' As usual there were no boring 'utility' shoes with flat heels in the Queen's wardrobe. So when the Queen found herself, several months later, gallantly trying in pretty high heels to scale the stony Matapos and view Cecil Rhodes' tomb, something had to be done. 'How like Mummy!' said Princess

En route to South Africa. The King and Queen stroll on the deck of the Vanguard *with Princess Elizabeth and Princess Margaret.*

Elizabeth delightedly, as she made the Queen wear her sandals and continued the climb in her stockings.

However strenuous things were to be in Southern Africa, they were worse in Britain. The appalling winter of 1946–7 had clamped down on the country. Even in the Home Counties the snow lay thick and frozen for nine solid weeks. There was a desperate fuel shortage. Not unexpectedly a few unpleasant remarks were made on the contrast between the Royal Family's visit to the sun and their people's visitation by the snow. A sovereign as conscientious and even thin-skinned as George VI could not but suffer from profound feelings of guilt. Nothing would have stopped him from turning around and going straight home again, to suffer with his people, had he not received contrary advice from the Prime Minister, Mr Attlee.

Queen Elizabeth explained the situation to Queen Mary on 9 March 1947, a month after they had started on 1 February:

This tour is being very strenuous as I feared it would be & doubly hard for Bertie who feels he should be at home. But there is very little he could do now, and even if he interrupted the tour and flew home, it would be very exhausting, & possibly make it difficult to return here. We think of home all the time, & Bertie has offered to return but Mr Attlee thought it would only make people think that things were getting worse & was not anxious for him to come back.

By the end of the tour the King had lost seventeen pounds in weight. He did not yet feel the cramps in his legs that were to be, alas, the beginning of the end, but these cramps were only months away. Two contrasting photographs again seem to point to the changes in his health. On Pretoria station, near the beginning of the tour, King George walks beside Field-Marshal Jan Smuts, both King and Prime Minister looking their best; King elegant in a white naval uniform and with the drawn look vanished; Smuts with his neat white beard, stick-up collar and shining shoes. Behind them the Queen raises her hand high in an enthusiastic greeting, while behind her walk her two daughters, Princess Elizabeth gazing round at the fascinating scene. Against this group must be set a most poignant but romantic profile of King George. It was 'snapped' towards the end of the tour by a South African student and has strange affinities with the famous profile of the poet Rupert Brooke. The King's features are clear-cut and taut – almost too taut for comfort – and his eyes have a faraway look. It is a profile to love, admire – and fear for.

Meanwhile the tour proved to be a many-faceted triumph. Thousands of miles were covered by road, air and rail, the last in the splendid royal 'White Train'. Lady Buxton who had been Governess-General of South Africa earlier in the century, once wrote home about the beauties of viceregal travel: 'I have never, I now know, travelled really comfortably before and I envy royalties who always travel in special trains.' But on this royal train, 1947 variety, the hours of comfort and relaxation were strictly limited. Lady Margaret Egerton was struck by the 'amazing stamina' of the Royal Family. 'They never could be sure even of a quiet meal on the train,' she recollects. 'Whenever the train stopped for coaling

ABOVE *The Queen borrows her daughter's shoes during the South African tour.*

BELOW *Snapshot of King George VI by a South African student.*

or water, crowds of blacks and whites would be there to greet them. Out would come the King and Queen, followed by the Princesses, on to the observation platform, whether they were in the middle of a meal or not.' Nor could the Queen hope to get away with the simple image of a beautifully dressed lady. She must look a *queen*. Another spectator remembers that voices would sometimes come from a crowd, 'Mrs Queen, Mrs Queen, where is your crown?'

Queen Elizabeth understands all this. She has always taken endless trouble, and will dress up at the most inconvenient moments, in order to adapt her own image to the glittering vision that people hold in their imaginations.

On the royal dining-table in the White Train was spread a tablecloth printed with the South African motto: '*Ex Unitate Vires*' – In Unity is Strength. The first time the King saw it he exclaimed, 'Not much unity here!' For when the King bestowed the Order of Merit upon Jan Smuts at Cape Town, many of the Nationalists stayed away. The King was shocked.

To insult Jan Smuts! Hero of the South African 'volk' in the Boer War, Smuts was now a great Imperial statesman. After one particularly virulent example in South Africa of dissension rather than unity, the King burst out characteristically, 'I'd like to shoot them all!' To which the Queen replied in her voice of gentle remonstrance, half smiling, 'But Bertie, you can't shoot *everybody*' – as though he could at least shoot *some*.

The King's sudden furies were possibly a hereditary part of his make-up, for George V, Edward VII and most of all the Duke of Teck had hot

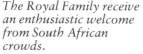

The Royal Family receive an enthusiastic welcome from South African crowds.

tempers. In the case of King George VI, however, his bursts of irritation were more likely to have developed through the frustrations of his youth, especially his stammer. Quite small annoyances out shooting or on the golf course would provoke what the Household had learnt to call one of HM's 'gnashes'. But the 'gnash' was over almost as soon as it had begun. The King never bore resentment.

'The Queen has a wonderful capacity for defusing a situation.' This is what people always remember about her. 'It is not just a technique but the sign of a deeply affectionate nature.' Her contribution in South Africa was typical of her quick wit and sympathy. When one of her Boer hosts confessed that he could never quite forgive the British for having conquered his country, Queen Elizabeth said, 'I understand that perfectly. We feel very much the same in Scotland.'

At the end of the tour many people, Smuts among them, felt that the South Africans, in taking the Royal Family to their hearts, had repudiated republicanism for ever. In fact, South Africa was to remain in the Commonwealth for only another fourteen years. Then, in 1961, 'the Great Trek' happened all over again. Dr Verwoerd led the *volk* out of the Commonwealth – and took all other South Africans, black, brown and white, with them.

As for the black Africans, their enthusiasm for the royal visit was vehement. One huge Zulu charged through a police cordon and made for the royal party. The Queen was greatly upset, fearing an attack on the Princesses. She later described it as 'the worst mistake in my life' when she tried to beat him off with her parasol. No one realized till

With General Smuts, Their Majesties and the Princesses in Natal's National Park.

'I declare before you all that my whole life ... shall be devoted to your service ...' From South Africa Princess Elizabeth broadcasts to the Commonwealth on her 21st birthday.

afterwards that he was offering Princess Elizabeth a ten-shilling note as a twenty-first birthday present.

The tour reached a happy climax on the eve of 21 April, Princess Elizabeth's birthday. It was four days before they were due to sail for England, and the Princess broadcast a message from Cape Town to all the peoples of the Commonwealth whose head she would some day become. Her theme was dedication:

I should like to make that dedication now. It is very simple. I declare before you all that my whole life, whether it be long or short, shall be devoted to your service and the service of our great Imperial Commonwealth to which we all belong ...

That moving dedication by the young Princess could have been spoken equally by either of her parents. The mention of a whole life, 'whether it be long or short', was to be tragically appropriate to her father.

The Queen and her family were not back in their own home until the end of the first week in May. This gave her under two months to arrange all the formalities and contact the many members of the two families, before she and her husband announced on 10 July the forthcoming marriage of their elder daughter. The date of the announcement happened to be the same as a Buckingham Palace garden party to which Harold Nicolson had been invited. 'It is raining slightly,' he wrote, adding patriotically, 'but I wear my top hat ... Everybody is straining to see the bridal pair – irreverently and shamelessly straining.'

The wedding itself was on 20 November 1947. 'Everybody' was to have an opportunity to see it without straining at all, whether irreverently or not, for the splendid procession and glorious interior of Westminster Abbey were filmed. It was also the first time in a decade that the excited crowds were able to cheer the Irish State coach attended by the Household Cavalry, in all their polished, jingling brilliance. Austerity was banished for the day.

As the bride stepped out of her golden coach on her father's arm, it seemed that a painting – Botticelli's *Primavera* – had come to life. The design for her wedding dress, described by James Laver as the 'poetry of dressmaking', included so many pearl and crystal garlands of York roses intertwined with ears of wheat, that the ivory satin had a faint glow of colour, though no colour was present.

Of course there had been the usual minor contretemps. Hartnell had ordered the silk for the thick satin train from Lullington Castle in Kent, but the finer silk for the satin dress he got from a Scottish firm in Dunfermline. Suddenly word went round that the Scots had used the products of 'enemy' silkworms, either Italian or Japanese. But when Hartnell telephoned Dunfermline he was told, 'Our worms are Chinese worms – from Nationalist China of course.'

While she was dressing, the Princess discovered that the necklace of pearls she intended to wear – a present from her parents – had been left behind at St James's Palace, where it was on display for charity with all the other wedding presents. How to reach it in time? A vast crowd was milling around the Palace. Jock Colville, the Princess's Private Secretary, fought his way through the crowds to St James's Palace and back again. His main difficulty was to convince the police of his *bona fides*.

It is said that Princess Elizabeth's bouquet was also mislaid at the last minute and retrieved from a refrigerator. She herself, like her mother before her, undoubtedly left her little white handkerchief bag in the State coach.

In his address the Archbishop of Canterbury pointed out that the Princess's wedding was 'in all essentials exactly the same as it would be for any cottager who might be married this afternoon in some small country church ...' This was what Walter Bagehot had meant when he said that a Royal Family at certain times, such as weddings, could lower their pride down to 'the level of petty life'.

Princess Elizabeth said the words, 'I will', with such conviction, wrote her father, that he knew 'everything was all right'. Just to make sure that everything was indeed all right Queen Elizabeth ordered a sprig of white heather from Balmoral to be placed beside the plate of every guest at the wedding breakfast. There were neither the interminable courses that there had been at her own wedding breakfast, nor long speeches.

The bridal pair began their honeymoon at Broadlands where, a month before, Princess Elizabeth had been a radiant bridesmaid at the wedding of Lady Patricia Mountbatten.

For the King, this great day had been a mixed blessing, and while

*Royal wedding 1947:
HRH The Princess
Elizabeth at Buckingham
Palace before her wedding
to Lt Philip Mountbatten,
RN.*

*Royal wedding 1947:
HRH The Princess
Elizabeth at Buckingham
Palace before her wedding
to Lt Philip Mountbatten,
RN.*

leading Lilibet up to the altar his face was a study in conflicting emotions. He certainly did not feel, as his great-grandmother Queen Victoria had felt when her eldest daughter was married: 'After all, it is like taking a poor Lamb to be sacrificed.' But the loss of Lilibet did come home to him in all its poignancy.

I was so proud of you [he wrote to her afterwards] & thrilled at having you so close to me on our long walk in Westminster Abbey, but when I handed your hand to the Archbishop I felt that I had lost something very precious ...

He found, however, that he had fortunately not lost Lilibet's confidence through postponing her engagement.

I am so glad [he went on] you wrote & told Mummy that you think the long wait before your engagement & the long time before the wedding was for the best. I was rather afraid that you thought I was being hard-hearted about it. I was so anxious for you to come to South Africa as you knew.

Then the King came to his simple but fervent family creed.

> Our family, us four, the 'Royal Family' must remain together with additions of course at suitable moments!! I have watched you grow up all these years under the skilful direction of Mummy, who as you know is the most marvellous person in the World in my eyes ...

The King had spoken of their 'long walk in Westminster Abbey'. He hoped still to walk a long way through life with Lilibet not too far off, teaching her the secrets of sovereignty.

As for the Queen, 'What a wonderful day it has been,' she said; 'they grow up and leave us and we must make the best of it.' That was *her* simple creed: to make the best of what life brought. She had said the same thing eleven years before when she reluctantly ascended the throne.

Life indeed went on busily and often pleasantly. True, the King could no longer sign himself 'George RI', for his Indian Empire of which he had been Rex Imperator had vanished; nor could the Queen avoid the duty of drinking cocktails with Molotov. 'We lean against the buffet,' wrote Nicolson on 3 December 1947, 'have champagne cocktails and watch Molotov talking to the Queen.' The best kind of Molotov cocktails had been in the war.

The Queen also organized all kinds of fun and games at home for her family and friends. 'Let's have a "Parada",' she would say, and the young men would dress up and goose-step past her and the King imitating a kind of Polish march-past, while she pretended to review them. Sir Stafford Cripps himself, the austere Labour Chancellor, would take part for, said a friend, 'she dissolves the whole atmosphere'.

Later it would be, 'Let's do the hokey-cokey'; or they would play 'Murder' (once there were two corpses, the second being an unwary visitor with a weak head); or 'Bringing in the Sentence', a game at which Lord ('Bobetty') Salisbury and Sir Arthur Penn the Queen's Treasurer were so skilful and witty that everyone hoped neither would bring the duel to an end by winning. Or she would play Racing Demon at which she was indeed a 'demon'; during one contest she asked Bobetty Salisbury how he was getting on, to which Bobetty replied with his engaging lisp, 'Oh, Ma'am, I am suwwounded by howwible, howwible Queens.'

At Christmas there was the Sandringham Carol Service, and present-tables for everybody in the ballroom on Christmas Eve. New Year's Eve had its own traditional ceremony: at midnight the youngest dark-haired footman knocked on the front door to bring the New Year in.

Picnics at Balmoral were always delicious and always the same: venison pâté, a chicken-and-ham filling inside what looked like penny buns with the tops cut off, and cold plum pudding. There was a bizarre moment at one shooting picnic when two dignified gentlemen wearing black City suits, bowler hats and town shoes – Lord Clarendon, the Lord Chamberlain, attended by Ernest Popplewell, a railwayman MP and Vice-Chamberlain – presented addresses to a King dressed in tweeds and attended by a retriever. Shooting could not be interrupted. In deference

to the King's taste, dinner at Balmoral also hardly varied from his favourite grouse *rôti à l'anglaise* and roast beef on Sundays.

But if the King's shooting could not be interrupted, the welfare and pleasure of his Household were always in the forefront of his mind. When one of his private secretaries had a first-born son the King said, 'I suppose you want me to be Godfather? Well, I will.' Another day he interrupted a game of charades to announce: 'We've been acting charades. Now we're going to act seriously'; and he proceeded to bestow the MVO on the Rector of Sandringham, the Reverend Hector Anderson ('Hector the Rector'), and the KCVO on Norman Gwatkin, Assistant Controller of the Lord Chamberlain's office. The King had brought down from London for the purpose a sword which the Coldstream Guards had presented to him, Gwatkin having been a Coldstreamer. He knighted Gwatkin there and then, who promptly bolted from the room, overcome by emotion.

Charades were always a standby and Queen Mary never failed to join in. One night she tied a napkin around her waist to play the part of a nurse in the word 'Operation'. Alas, it was soon to be a word of ill-omen.

The Queen already knew that King George was suffering cramps in both his legs. Nevertheless 1948 was a joyous year for Queen Elizabeth and her husband. On 26 April they celebrated their silver wedding, and on 14 November their first grandchild Prince Charles was born.

Their wedding anniversary began with a Thanksgiving Service at St Paul's, followed by a twenty-mile drive through beflagged London Streets, all day in the April sunshine.

The King and Queen both broadcast, rededicating themselves to their people. It was through 'my home', said the King, that he found the strength to serve, during what John Masefield the Poet Laureate called 'these cruel years'.

The Queen also made her theme for the Jubilee the homes of others. 'Looking back over the last twenty-five years,' she said, 'and to my own happy childhood, I realize more and more the wonderful sense of security and happiness which comes from a loved home.' Her heart went out to the people who were still waiting for 'a home of their own'. She had seen so many homes go down; now she wanted to see new ones go up. Homes and families were in miniature the 'secret of community' which the world sought.

By October the King's cramps were painful and permanent. In the same month that her grandson was born – November – the Queen learnt from the doctors that her husband had early arteriosclerosis, with danger of gangrene and of the amputation of his right leg. Her outward serenity and cheerfulness helped him to make a partial recovery, but in March 1949 a thrombosis caused his doctors to insist on an operation. It was in this very March that he and the Queen had planned a fresh tour of Australia and New Zealand. Instead he underwent a right lumbar sympathectomy.

OPPOSITE *A dramatic photograph by Cecil Beaton of HM Queen Elizabeth at Buckingham Palace in 1948.*

BELOW *The King and Queen with Prince Charles and Princess Anne on the Prince's third birthday, November 1951.*

ABOVE *The Royal Family attend a gala evening at a London theatre.*

LEFT *Although seriously ill, the King stands bareheaded on the tarmac of Heathrow Airport waving farewell to Princess Elizabeth. The Queen and Princess Margaret stand behind him.*

Again he seemed to recover and the tour was re-planned for spring 1952, the Festival of Britain being already scheduled for 1951. Human affection and the people's concern buoyed him up; but Britain's economic plight beat him down. 'What I fear is another 1931 crisis,' he wrote five months after his operation; and next year he was further depressed by the Korean War. 'The incessant worries & crises through which we have to live', he wrote in 1951, 'got me down properly.'

But he did not have to live through them much longer. The Queen in autumn 1951 followed her husband, again seriously ill, home from Balmoral. For the first time she could not face the anxious crowds and drove into Buckingham Palace by a side entrance. When the King had a second operation, on 23 September, she knew, though he did not, that it was for cancer of the lung. His old enemy, a fatal thrombosis, still hung over him and indeed drew rapidly nearer. Yet she kept her own counsel, as she had during the dark days of the war, seeming calmly occupied as ever.

Three-year-old Prince Charles and one-year-old Princess Anne were in her charge while their parents toured Canada and America. She was nurse-in-chief to the King. And at Christmas she gave presents to the Sandringham people on the King's behalf. One of the cleaners found herself saying how much they all loved the Queen. 'You're the sort of person, Ma'am, we'd like to have for a neighbour.'

The King's doctor gave permission for him to see off Philip and Lilibet on a planned Commonwealth tour in the New Year, 1952. He himself was encouraged to dream of convalescing in South Africa that March. On 30 January the whole family went to see *South Pacific*. Next day the King looked on Lilibet for the last time, from the tarmac at London Airport. Five days later he was shooting on a glorious winter day at Sandringham, while the Queen and Princess Margaret drove over to Edward Seago's at Ludham for a cruise on the Norfolk Broads and to bring back some of Seago's paintings to show the King. Margaret played the piano to him before he went to sleep, while Queen Elizabeth listened. A moving pattern of history seemed to be repeating itself. Princess Alice had played to her dying father, Prince Albert, while Queen Victoria listened. Albert's great-grandson and namesake fell asleep about midnight on 5 February, and it was in his sleep during the early hours of the 6th that he died.

In the King's last Christmas broadcast (recorded in short periods, as his voice allowed) he had no longer felt compelled to speculate on the nation's future, but turned with his whole heart to what would remain changeless – the human family. 'At Christmas we feel that the old simple things matter most,' he said. 'They do not change, however much the world outside may seem to do so.'

Now, in one brief and tragic moment, the whole world outside had indeed changed for Queen Elizabeth.

Mother of The Queen

7

T HE KING'S DEATH was a shattering blow to Queen Elizabeth, even
though for the past four years she had known that his health was fail-
ing. Her extraordinary fortitude in facing this catastrophe must not blind
us to the sharpness of her tragedy. For many weeks she found the solitude
of her own thoughts almost unbearable. And yet she could not bring herself to invite friends to visit her. Years later Peter Cazalet, the brilliantly
successful trainer of her horses, was to die of cancer. His widow Zara
remembers Queen Elizabeth's total understanding of her misery, her
feeling of being utterly 'bowled over', so that at times the laughter of her
own grown-up children jarred. It is permissible to guess that Queen
Elizabeth had known these feelings herself.

Nevertheless she was still a Queen, if a Queen Widow. There were
things to be done, decisions to be taken. One of her first instinctive acts
was to turn to the guilelessness of small children; not for oblivion – that
was impossible – but for the momentary suspense of suffering. She called
to mind the lines of the poet William Blake that she had seen on the
annual report of the North Islington Infant Welfare Centre:

Labour well the minute particulars, attend to the little ones,
And those who are in misery cannot remain so, long.

So she played as usual with Prince Charles and Princess Anne, two
laughing under-fives, while their parents were flying home.

Otherwise she would sit at her desk composing letters and drawing up
a message to the nation. Her message, a moving thank-you in reply to all
the sympathy she had received, was exceptionally felicitous even for her:

I want you to know how your concern for me has upheld me in my sorrow,
and how proud you have made me by your wonderful tribute to my dear
husband, a great and noble King.

'Noble' was exactly the right word. To show nobility of character in a life
full of ordeals and difficulties is a rare thing. King George VI displayed
that combination of high-mindedness, dedication and self-sacrifice that
makes up true nobility.

The Queen Mother concluded her message with her own re-
dedication:

My only wish now is that I may be allowed to continue the work that we
sought to do together.

OPPOSITE *A formal
photograph of Queen
Elizabeth the Queen
Mother as Her Majesty
had now become.*

*'One cannot yet believe
that it has all happened.'
Awaiting the King's coffin
at Westminster Hall, left
to right, the new Queen,
Queen Mary, Queen
Elizabeth and Princess
Margaret.*

As we shall see, the Queen Mother has not only continued their work but
extended it over the course of a most fruitful second span that is
approaching thirty years.

One of the Queen Mother's letters to a friend has been published. It
was written to Ted Seago, the painter who had given so much pleasure to
the royal couple on their last day together.

I got back rather late [she wrote to Seago] and, as I always did, rushed straight to the King's room to say that I was back and to see how he was. I found him so well, so gay . . . and then I told him that you had sent the pictures back in my car and we went straight to the hall where they had been set out . . .

We had such a truly gay dinner with the King, like his old self, and more picture looking after dinner . . . One cannot yet believe that it has all happened, one feels rather dazed . . .

The return of her daughter, now Queen Elizabeth II, from Kenya, brought home the sad fact that it really had 'all happened'. The dramatic setting in which the new Queen received the news of her father's death is now well known. It was broken to her by her husband, after she had spent a magical night in the branches of a gigantic fig at the Tree Tops Hotel, watching many wild animals coming down to drink at a water-hole, and two bucks fighting for mastery of their kingdom. There were to be no conflicts over the passing of the kingdom to Elizabeth II, such as had marred the Accession of her father. Nevertheless many changes were necessary, one being in the royal names.

Queen Elizabeth II was henceforth known by this title, or more shortly as 'The Queen'. Since her mother has the same Christian name as herself, it has been essential to distinguish them. The Household's adoption of the title 'Queen Elizabeth' for the Queen Mother will also be followed in this book. Otherwise Queen Elizabeth will be called 'The Queen Mother' – but never 'The Dowager Queen'. That portentous title fits neither her nor the age in which she lives.

Another change was in the royal homes. At the time of the King's death, Queen Elizabeth was living with her husband and unmarried daughter Margaret in Buckingham Palace, while Princess Elizabeth, *her* husband and two children lived a few hundred yards along the Mall at Clarence House. In this case there was to be a simple exchange of London homes. The reigning Sovereign and her family moved at once into Buckingham Palace, while Queen Elizabeth and Princess Margaret were to occupy Clarence House as soon as it was ready for them. The date was to be 18 May 1953.

In the English countryside the changes were even simpler. The Queen Mother spent her weekends and as much other time as possible in her beloved Royal Lodge, the Queen and her family occupying Windsor Castle and Sandringham. On Deeside, Balmoral became the Queen's Scottish castle; and Birkhall, lying seven miles distant on the river Muick, was again her mother's cherished Highland home. But in the far north of Scotland there was to be a quite new development.

Queen Elizabeth was resting quietly with her devoted friends, Commander Clare and Lady Doris Vyner, on the Vyners' remote Caithness estate romantically called 'The House of the Northern Gate'. By chance she heard that a small sixteenth-century castle on the Pentland Firth was up for sale. Curiosity about things, especially people and houses, has always been a secret of Queen Elizabeth's charm, or so says Lady Salisbury, one of her oldest friends. To visit someone's house is for her the perfect climax to any expedition or picnic. The young Queen

Victoria and many other royal ladies have also shared this interest in house viewing.

And thus Queen Elizabeth found herself visiting little Barrogill, once the fortress home of the Earls of Caithness. It still had intact its massive stone walls, turrets, enclosed jungly gardens and two small squat cannon drawn up under its windows. It even boasted an older romantic name dating from a remote past – Mey, the Castle of Mey.

There was an empty place in Queen Elizabeth's heart, and the little Scots castle immediately filled it. What would its likely fate be? she asked. Demolition, in all probability, for there had been no bids. 'Pull it down? Never! I'll buy it!' said the widowed Queen, to whom saving a life, if only that of a castle, seemed infinitely worthwhile. Her Majesty bought Barrogill, changed its name back to Mey, and set in train the long but satisfyingly creative process of making it habitable. The first home of her own that Queen Elizabeth had ever possessed, Mey also offered her 'a room with a view' – a wide wild view from her sitting-room window right over the tossing Firth to the Orkneys, on a clear day. Inside, the Queen Mother put neat rush matting and a tartan hearthrug beneath her sitting-room's white walls and red curtains. Outside Mother Nature had put two whirlpools, the locally nicknamed 'Swirlies' and 'Twirlies'.

How did all these house-moving and home-making operations affect the Queen Mother's recovery from the first agony of bereavement? It is said that a widow should not have to make too sudden and abrupt an exit from her old home. The Queen Mother did not move into Clarence House until over a year after the King's death and only a fortnight before her daughter's Coronation. At the same time, if a widow can somehow create a new aspect of her life entirely unconnected with the past, that will be a positive step towards recovery. At the Castle of Mey Queen Elizabeth did just this. She found at first privacy and peace. But the privacy and peace led in due course to activity and enterprise, in the shape of a pedigree herd of Aberdeen Angus cattle, a small flock of sheep, marketable flowers, vegetables and fruit, and her own special harvest of fish from the River Thurso.

Before the Coronation on 2 June 1953, another landmark from the old life was to go. The death of Queen Mary, who was nearly eighty-six years old, occurred on 24 March. 'Queen Mary died at 10.20,' wrote Harold Nicolson in his diary, 'and Winston announces it in sobs at 10.45.' The Duke of Windsor was at her bedside, but not of course his Duchess. Since his mother had never consented to receive his wife, such a visit would have been inappropriate.

Queen Mary had always backed up Queen Elizabeth loyally and the younger widow was to miss her sadly. Despite her temperamental rigidity and painful shyness, Queen Mary belonged to the same 'royal trades union' as Queen Elizabeth – to adopt King George VI's expression. It was a trade union that existed to protect its members' rights, and also to keep up standards. By no means did it believe in a closed shop for royalty. But there were rules. And one of them was a rule against divorce.

The first divorce to affect this generation of the Royal Family had

The castle that the Queen Mother transformed into a home – The Castle of Mey in Northern Scotland.

happened, paradoxically, outside it. This was the decree absolute granted in December 1952 to Peter Townsend, on the grounds of his wife Rosemary's adultery. He was the innocent party. Just as Wallis Simpson had been.

We know from Mrs Belloc Lowndes, who had many friends at Court, that when Queen Mary heard her son David intended to marry Wallis Simpson, she wept and spent many nights and days sleepless and unable to eat. When, two months before the Coronation, the Queen Mother had to tell her Household that Princess Margaret and Peter Townsend intended to marry, she too, like Queen Mary, burst into tears for the first and last time in their memory.

Nevertheless Peter Townsend wrote in his memoirs, *Time and Chance*, 'The Queen Mother listened [to their declaration] with characteristic understanding ... without a sign that she felt angered or outraged – or that she acquiesced – and the Queen Mother was never anything but considerate in her attitude to me. She never once hurt either of us throughout the whole difficult affair.'

Of course this was true; it was not in her character to hurt anyone, certainly not her deeply loved and admired daughter and a devoted servant of her Household (Townsend had been with her since the King's death, and with the King since 1944 after a brilliant war in the RAF, and was now Deputy Master of the Household.) How much it hurt *her* was another question.

Margaret had recently lost an adored father who spoilt her. Owing to the war, she had been allowed to stay up for dinner on occasion ever since

The royal ladies walking at Balmoral. With them is Group-Captain Peter Townsend.

she was twelve. In return she would reward the grown-ups by being 'outrageously funny' – a gift which her grandmother Queen Mary admitted they could not resist encouraging. Margaret was also adept at defusing a situation. One evening, for instance, something had upset the King and it looked as if a 'gnash' was in danger of developing. Princess Margaret, however, had the mischievous idea of suddenly throwing her spoon over her shoulder. Everyone's attention was distracted and the 'gnash' dissolved in laughter.

Queen Elizabeth depended almost as much as the King had done on her charming daughter's companionship and wit. For in many ways, Princess Margaret's talents for mimicry were the same as her mother's in youth. If ever a Glamis party showed signs of dragging, someone would say, 'Where's Elizabeth? Send for her.' Similarly a close friend recalls occasions when Queen Elizabeth wondered rather anxiously whether a certain party would go. 'But Margaret will be there,' she would remember with relief. 'It will be quite all right.'

There is little doubt that, but for the Townsend divorce, Princess Margaret would have been given permission to marry the man she loved. Permission? The word sounds strangely out of place as applied to marriage in our present permissive society, and was somewhat anachronistic even a quarter of a century ago, but it still applies to the marriages of all King George II's descendants in the royal line. The Royal Marriages Act of 1772 was an attempt to save the throne from the dubious fancies of George III's sons, and as such perhaps was justifiable. The burden that it imposed 180 years later upon the young Queen Elizabeth II was neither necessary nor humane. If ever the appropriate moment arrives, this Act should be repealed.

Meanwhile, the two hard-pressed royal ladies, Queen Elizabeth and her daughter the Queen, could be forgiven if they hoped that the problem would go away. After all, Princess Margaret was only twenty-two. Group-Captain Townsend was thirty-eight – sixteen years older than the Princess. There was already a 'Margaret set' of dashing and acceptable young men. Might she still not fall for one of them?

If the problem of the engagement would not go away, perhaps Peter himself would do so? His peculiar combination of father-figure and suitor would be desperately missed by the Princess, while his charm and efficiency would leave a blank at Clarence House, where he was now Comptroller of the Queen Mother's Household. Nevertheless, it would have been the best solution, and he was indeed offered quite early in the day an opportunity in Kuwait. But his own concept of honour and his sense of obligation to the Princess prevented him from accepting.

By the time Coronation Day dawned on 2 June 1953 there had been no decision. As Princess Margaret and Group-Captain Townsend stood waiting under the dripping awning outside the Abbey's west door, an alert Press noticed them laughing and talking together, wrapped away in that dream of 'another world which belonged, jointly and exclusively to us' – to quote Townsend again. The Press observed the Princess examining the war hero's rows of medals and flicking a speck of dust from his uniform. From such a speck was to grow the Press campaign that broke less than two weeks later.

Fortunately for Queen Elizabeth she could not foresee this disastrous development. For her the Coronation was doubly moving, since her daughter the Queen was now experiencing the same sense of religious dedication that she herself had felt sixteen years before. Like Queen Mary, she attended her successor's ceremony, the second Queen Mother to do so. The people picked her out for special cheering, while the diarists gave her frequent mention. Harold Nicolson, it is true, roguishly put the Queen Mother's glass coach on a par, for interest, with the horse ambulance that brought up the rear. Anne Edwards of the *Daily Express*, however, caught the authentic note in describing Queen Elizabeth's processing up the Abbey, to the thunderous organ beat of William Walton's *Orb and Sceptre*:

On she came up the aisle with a bow here to Prince Bernhard, a bow there to the row of ambassadors, and up those tricky steps with no looking down like the Duke of Goucester, no half turn to check on her train like the Duchess of Kent, no hesitation at the top like Princess Margaret, no nervous nods of her head like Princess Mary. She is the only woman I ever saw who can slow up naturally when she sees a camera.

The 'no-looking-down' technique had been taught to her by her mother Lady Strathmore, who had said, 'Never look at your feet.' As for Princess Marina's 'half-turn to check on her train', this reminds one of the celebrated contrast between the Empress Eugénie and Queen Victoria when taking their seats in the royal box at the theatre. Whereas Eugénie would always look back over her shoulder before sitting down, to make sure there was a chair to sit down upon, Victoria, 'bred to the purple', took the chair for granted. She never looked back or down. The strange thing about Queen Elizabeth was that she was not 'bred to the purple' and yet she had acquired these royal graces.

Another diarist, Cecil Beaton, the incomparable photographer and designer, was present. He noted that even the towering height of the Mistress of the Robes was 'minimized by the enormous presence and radiance of the petite Queen Mother'. Beaton, however, saw beyond the radiance. 'Yet in the Queen Widow's expression,' he added, 'we read sadness combined with pride.'

Queen Elizabeth watched the familiar ceremony from the front row of the Royal Gallery. At Queen Alexandra's Coronation there had been what was known as the 'Loose Box' above the Royal Gallery: a special box devoted to King Edward's 'loose' lady friends. There was no 'Loose Box' at Elizabeth II's Coronation, because there were no high-stepping mares around to occupy it. But a small pony trotted into the Royal enclosure just before the Queen's Crowning. It was Prince Charles, aged four, in a white satin suit, with sleek shining hair. He squeezed in between his Aunt Margaret and his Grandmother, and proceeded to show an interest in the pageantry. Queen Elizabeth maintained a judicious balance between answering his whispered questions and keeping him quiet with a rummage in her handbag.

As ever, the glorious moment of the Crowning put all the diarists on their mettle. Chips Channon saw the white arms of the peeresses lifting up their coronets as so many beautiful curving swans' necks; but Cecil Beaton thought they resembled something rather less romantic – 'The peeresses with long gloved arms,' he wrote, 'looking like wishbones.' It was Cecil Beaton also who spotted the slight hitch in which the Queen Mother was involved while about to process from the Abbey at the end. 'Someone has mistakenly allowed minor members of the clergy to go before her,' wrote Beaton; 'a herald is sent to inform her of what has happened. She smiles patiently as she waits.' Curiously, a fainting clergyman had held her up at her own Coronation.

Cecil Beaton came into his own when the royal photographs were afterwards taken at Buckingham Palace. He has given an enchanting human sketch of the agreeably chaotic scene.

He had buoyed himself up during the early, shivering hours of waiting in the Abbey with a panacea for nerves that the Queen Mother herself would have highly approved – 'eating barley sugar (very sustaining) . . .' The Queen Mother had long ago discovered the saving powers of a toffee or mint. She once tossed a 'sustaining' cube to a policeman.

A cool head and steady hand were required for this photographic

LEFT *The Queen Mother with her grandson at her daughter's Coronation.*

BELOW *The newly crowned Sovereign together with her children, Prince Philip and the Queen Mother watch the Coronation fly-past from Buckingham Palace.*

OPPOSITE *Wearing the diamond base of her own crown, the Queen Mother photographed with her grandson by Cecil Beaton after the Coronation.*

session at the Palace. Beaton had managed to snatch an hour's sleep at home between the Coronation service and the return of the Royal Family to the Palace, while the Family had been driving through the streets in their State coaches, to arrive home at last, exhilarated and exhausted. No time for a rest. But the Queen Mother, at least, seemed one who did not require a rest. Beaton heard a group of Palace servants raise a tremendous cheer, as her glass coach bowled through the central arch with the Queen Mother inside 'waving and smiling as fresh as a field flower'.

The Palace servants' enthusiasm was genuine; when Queen Elizabeth had left Buckingham Palace for Clarence House a fortnight before, all the Palace servants wanted to go with her.

Cecil Beaton was to photograph the family first, and the Queen after she had been taken by *The Times* in the Throne Room. He could hear the laughter, jokes and high-pitched voices echoing from the Picture Gallery. Everyone was keyed-up, especially the Queen's two small, excited children.

As the Queen Mother, 'dimpled and chuckling, with eyes as bright as any of her jewels', came towards him, accompanied by Princess Margaret, Beaton could see that Prince Charles and Princess Anne were determined to get hold of Princess Margaret's long purple train. The Princess's four pages gallantly fended them off, whereupon the children ran round and round the train-bearers making attacks on the train. At last they both dived underneath it.

Taking photographs was a hit or miss affair. No time to lose. 'Please turn this way, now that ... Quick, quick!' The Duke of Edinburgh put his head round a mirrored door and summoned Beaton's group into the rival 'studio' – the Throne Room. 'But you must come! You're keeping the whole group waiting!' Unhurried as ever, the Queen Mother sailed away, attended by her flotilla of pages and grandchildren. Cecil Beaton was left disconsolate. A little later, however, he was able to continue his account.

Then the return of the Queen Mother in rollicking spirits, and a slow voice asking: 'Do you really want to take a few more?' Suddenly I felt as if all my anxieties and fears were dispelled. The Queen Mother, by being so basically human and understanding, gives out to us a feeling of reassurance. The great mother figure and nannie to us all, through the warmth of her sympathy bathes us and wraps us in a counterpane by the fire-side.

She anchored her grandchildren in her arms, since both were buzzing about in the wildest excitement, refusing to keep still even for the snap-second of a photograph. Beaton saw 'a terrific picture' as she bent her head down to kiss Prince Charles's hair.

Suddenly I had this wonderful accomplice – someone who would help me through everything. All at once, and because of her, I was enjoying my work.

One important point about Beaton's unique recollection of the Coronation is his realization of how much the Queen owed to the Queen Mother. Among many of her mother's traits, she had inherited the frank

serenity of her eyes – 'not those of a busy, harassed person'. And her mother had taught her also 'never to use a superfluous gesture'. All these graces had been handed down to the Queen Mother by *her* mother. The royal ladies from whom she had learnt as a young bride had been able to teach her protocol but not spontaneity. Queen Mary, for all her honest goodness, had never been able to 'smile in public', wrote Cecil Beaton, 'or look anyone straight in the face.'

Twelve days after the Coronation the crisis of Princess Margaret's engagement broke. It forced upon the Queen Mother and her two daughters a complex evaluation of their duties to the Crown and to one another. Queen Elizabeth, in particular, would have to weigh up two 'goods' in the balance: her duty to promote Princess Margaret's happiness, versus her duty to help uphold the sanctity of marriage through the example of the Royal Family. Her own feelings and those of the Queen were strongly against divorce, as a threat to family life.

Then there was Parliament's reaction to consider. It was only sixteen years since Parliament had prevented a king from placing a divorced woman beside him on the throne. Would Parliament now allow a King's daughter, third in succession, to make a divorced man her consort?

The *News of the World* first published the story of the Princess and the Group-Captain. Their light-hearted conversation outside the Abbey had already been reported in the foreign press. Now it erupted at home, to darken or brighten – whichever way one looked at it – a British Sunday on 14 June 1953.

The immediate need was for the Queen to consult her Prime Minister. Winston Churchill had of course been a 'King's man' in 1936; he had seen no good reason why King Edward VIII should not marry the woman of his choice. Churchill was a romantic. Therefore it was not surprising that his immediate reaction, at the Chequers luncheon table, was again a romantic one. He beamed, and began stringing together some colourful and characteristic thoughts. 'What a delightful match! A lovely young royal lady married to a gallant young airman, safe from the perils and horrors of war!'

But his wife Clementine overheard the oration. She leant across the table. 'Winston,' she said, 'if you are going to begin the Abdication all over again, I'm going to leave! I shall take a flat and go and live in Brighton.'

Mary Soames's absorbing and invaluable life of her mother, *Clementine*, recounts how often Lady Churchill tried to change her famous husband's mind, and how sometimes she succeeded. In this particular case her reaction against the marriage was shared by a powerful section of the Cabinet. Lord Salisbury, for instance, held strong religious views on divorce and the Church. His father before him, and indeed the whole influential Cecil family, had steadfastly opposed the idea of a twice-divorced Queen in the form of Wallis Simpson. Sixteen years later the then Lord Salisbury felt he could not remain in a Cabinet which approved the marriage of Princess Margaret to a divorcee.

In advising the Queen, therefore, Churchill had to bear in mind that, whatever courses were legally open to the Royal Family, neither the Cabinet nor, probably, Parliament would ever sanction the marriage.

The legal options were straightforward. Since the Queen in present circumstances could not give the permission required by the Royal Marriages Act, her sister must wait until she was twenty-five. She would then be legally entitled to marry whom she chose – after notifying Parliament of her intention. But here was a catch. Parliament would need a further year in which to consider the marriage and register approval or otherwise. If Parliament disapproved – as appeared more than likely – Princess Margaret's marriage to Townsend would be an extremely expensive pleasure. For Parliament could strike her out of the line of succession and hence off the Civil List. She would have no official income and would lose her rank and status. Furthermore, Townsend had no fortune of his own, while Princess Margaret had no career but the royal one, which would henceforth be closed to her. In view of these facts, the royal statute of 1772 could better be described as an Anti-Marriage Act.

It seems doubtful whether the Royal Family fully realized the pincer movement which was being operated against the doomed pair and would inevitably crush their hopes. Princess Margaret was advised to see nothing of Townsend for the requisite two years. He left the royal service, having been given the post of British Air Attaché in Belgium. The two continued to correspond and evidently looked forward to marriage after August 1955, when Princess Margaret would attain the age of twenty-five.

One can imagine the tense atmosphere at Clarence House over those years: the Queen Mother loving and hoping – but for what? Her daughter hoping also, but assailed by doubts from every side. Would such a marriage help the Royal Family? (Margaret was fanatically loyal.) Was it in accord with her own, her mother's and her sister's religious beliefs? Would it work, particularly if she were cut off from the Royal Family by Act of Parliament?

At last the nerve-racking period of waiting came to an end. Peter Townsend, now forty-one, returned from Belgium. But a disconcerting piece of news had already been delivered by the new Prime Minister, Sir Anthony Eden. A majority in Parliament would almost certainly find the marriage unacceptable. In the light of this discouragement, to put it mildly, he and the Queen Mother, and afterwards he and Princess Margaret met for talks in Clarence House. The Princess's moving words of renunciation were the final result.

I would like it to be known [she announced] that I have decided not to marry Group-Captain Townsend. I have been aware that, subject to my renouncing my rights of succession, it might be possible for me to contract a civil marriage. But mindful of the Church's teaching that Christian marriage is indissoluble, and conscious of my duty to the Commonwealth, I have resolved to put these considerations before others . . .

Peter Townsend tells us that he drafted this statement for her the night before the announcement. Others suggest that her friend the Reverend

Simon Phipps, or even the Archbishop of Canterbury helped her reach
her self-sacrificing decision. One may perhaps assume that her mother's
influence was equally if not more potent, since Queen Elizabeth's own
simple but powerful faith has always kept her close to the Church's
thinking.

No one can doubt that the ordeal of this broken romance added to the
sorrow of Queen Elizabeth's early widowhood. The question has often
been asked, would it have happened if King George VI had been alive?
Such a hypothetical question is difficult to answer, except perhaps from
one angle. It is possible that Peter Townsend might have thought twice
before asking his Sovereign for his daughter's hand. Townsend knew
about 'gnashes', none better. And this time there would have been a

gnash to end gnashes, and even the beguiling Princess could not have tossed up a silver spoon high enough to charm it away.

Another frequent question is, why did not the King and Queen see the affair coming, and terminate Townsend's royal employment, instead of constantly renewing it? This argument overlooks the special nature of royalty. It would never have entered the King's head that his equerry could aspire to his daughter's hand. Even to suspect such a thing would have meant that the King and Queen had begun living in a different world from the royal world of the fifties. Some might say they ought to have begun to do so. But that would be asking King George and Queen Elizabeth to be entirely different people from the two we know. And that was surely not what the nation wanted.

By the time Queen Elizabeth was sadly left alone to deal with family problems, and Peter Townsend was free to marry, her daughter was twenty-three. This is not an age at which daughters expect their mothers to be heavy-handed. Or if they are, it may be counter-productive. Most parents would have acted as the Queen Mother did. And despite all the unhappiness, the Royal Family has remained as close as ever.

A happy ending for all seemed to come about at the end of the fifties. In 1959 Peter Townsend re-married. Princess Margaret fell in love with a young star of the photographic world, Antony Armstrong-Jones. Though he was a commoner, that question was not raised. But a curious glance at his pedigree on his beautiful mother's side would have revealed

Driving to her younger daughter's wedding, Her Majesty shared Queen Alexandra's State Coach with the Queen and Prince Charles.

Princess Margaret with her bridegroom, Anthony Armstrong-Jones, after their wedding at Westminster Abbey, 6 May 1960.

a recurrent gleam of brilliance – Messels, Sambournes (Linley Sambourne was a famous *Punch* artist) and the three Linley sisters – one of whom ran off with the playwright Sheridan – who caused all their male contemporaries to lose their heads. Princess Margaret and Lord Snowdon (as Tony Armstrong-Jones had been created) were married in Westminster Abbey on 6 May 1960. Four years later this family had presented the Queen Mother with two more delightful grandchildren: David, Viscount Linley, and his sister Lady Sarah Armstrong-Jones. And Princess Margaret, as we shall see, would continue to provide her mother with all the hopes and disappointments that are in the gift of a sparkling but volatile personality.

From the moment of her widowhood, Queen Elizabeth had found nothing but reassurance and consolation in her elder daughter and her family. It is said the Queen and her mother telephoned each other every day unless they met.

Prince Charles has always held a special place in Queen Elizabeth's affections by reason of his being the first grandchild, and in some ways the son she never had. The King had known and loved him as a friendly three-year-old, 'too sweet, stumping about the room', while staying at Sandringham under his grandparents' care. There was also a temperamental bond between Charles and his grandmother. 'He has *heart*,' says an old friend of both. 'He really feels things *here*' – putting his hand over his heart – 'exactly like Queen Elizabeth. He felt the death of Dickie [Lord Mountbatten] most terribly; it was not just tragic, it *hurt*.'

Such tender feelings about others usually mean a vulnerable personality, and Queen Elizabeth has recognized this characteristic in her eldest grandson. Prince Charles may indeed have inherited his compassion and sensibility from *both* his grandparents, since King George VI was always stirred by the sufferings of wrong-doers as well as of victims. He followed all courts-martial in a merciful spirit, and tried more than once to make Herbert Morrison (Home Secretary) commute a death sentence.

Taking her grandson's character into account, Queen Elizabeth would probably have preferred him to go to school at Eton for the same reason that his parents thought it inadvisable – because Eton was so very near home. But it was also too near to London and the Press. Queen Elizabeth has always been exceptionally good with the Press, and her tendency to think the best of everyone may have led her to hope that the Press would not badger Prince Charles even were he at Eton. When I asked another friend to explain her special feeling for Charles, he replied, 'I expect she was sorry for the poor boy, being sent to that terrible school in the mountains.' Few would recognize Gordonstoun in that unflattering description. Nevertheless, his grandmother did visit Charles there most assiduously, taking him and his friends out at half-term and no doubt sharing with them her bag of favourite toffees.

She felt some counterbalance was needed to the process of toughening. The telephone wires between Birkhall and Gordonstoun were often red-hot, Charles being summoned with the words, 'Granny's on the line!' And she managed to make one of her world tours coincide with Charles's first term at Timbertop in Australia. There was a joyous meeting between the two at Canberra airport.

Prince Charles's worship of his grandmother does not stop short 'this side of idolatry'. In a glowing Foreword to Godfrey Talbot's biography of *Queen Elizabeth The Queen Mother*, Prince Charles wrote:

I can only admit from the very start that I am hopelessly biased and completely partisan ... Ever since I can remember my grandmother has been the most wonderful example of fun, laughter, warmth, infinite security ... For me she has always been one of those extraordinarily rare people whose touch can turn everything to gold —

Among the skills that Prince Charles owes to her is a mastery of fly-fishing, taught him in Scotland. Quite properly, the pupil has now

Prince Charles and his fiancée Lady Diana Spencer, daughter of Earl Spencer and granddaughter of Ruth, Lady Fermoy, the Queen Mother's great friend and Lady-in-waiting. This particular marriage to a girl full of character and from a historic family like the Queen Mother herself, is what his grandmother has wished for above all things.

overtaken the teacher and Charles is the best fisherman in the family.

The announcement of his engagement on 24 February 1981 and marriage in July to Lady Diana Spencer has given pleasure to his grandmother.

Princess Anne's striking looks, her dynamism and devotion to horses have always made a direct appeal to Queen Elizabeth. Particularly while Princess Anne was a boarder at Benenden School, Kent, and her grandmother's horses were being trained at Fairlawne not far away, they saw a great deal of one another. If a helicopter was being used to take Queen Elizabeth to a duty in the neighbourhood, the visit might be combined with a look-in at Benenden.

1960 brought another grandson, Prince Andrew, last but one of the Queen's family. His handsome appearance pleased not only his grandmother but Harold Nicolson as well. 'Prince Andrew looks a nice baby,' he wrote to his wife on 23 March, having just seen the first photographs published since Andrew's birth on 19 February. 'He looks like a person already, not like a poached-egg like most new-born babies.

The announcement that the Queen was to have another baby had been

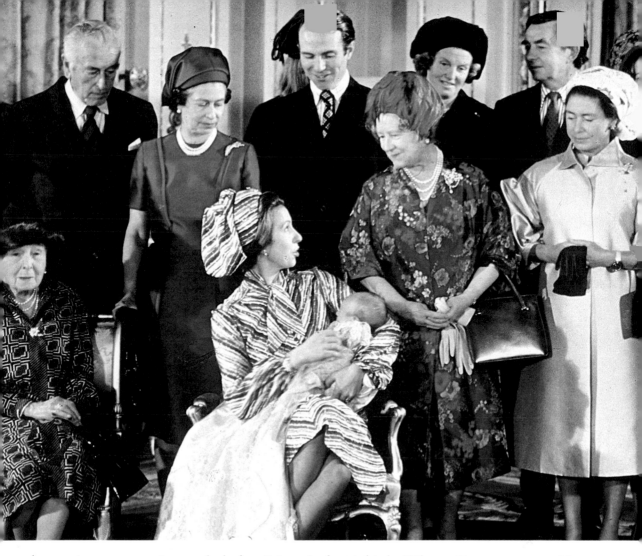

made on 7 August 1959, six months before Prince Andrew's birth. 'What a sentimental hold the monarchy has over the middle classes!' Nicolson had written in his diary on that day. 'All the solicitors, actors and publishers of the Garrick were beaming as if they had acquired some personal benefit.'

The later photographs of Prince Andrew with his grandmother show that Queen Elizabeth was beaming with the best of them, for she did acquire a personal benefit with the birth of every grandchild.

She had found other ways, however, beyond the family, of building up her life again from the desolation left by her early loss of the King. One all-important path was that of public work. This is an impressive side of the Queen Mother's character and deserves a chapter to itself. The years since the death of George VI are the story of a triumphant transformation, when the grandmother in turn of Charles, Anne, Andrew, David, Edward and Sarah, and the great-grandmother of Peter Phillips, Princess Anne's first-born, was also to become the people's 'Queen Mum'.

Five generations of the Royal Family gather at the christening of Princess Anne's son – from Queen Victoria's granddaughter, Princess Alice, Countess of Athlone, to Peter Phillips, 1977.

Second Flowering

8

T HE QUEEN MOTHER was once asked about the widowhood of Princess Victoria, 1st Marchioness of Milford Haven. 'It was such a long widowhood. Thirty years alone. How did she fill in her life?' The Queen Mother who, as we have seen, looked after this royal widow at Windsor during the war, knew the answers. 'Her family were terribly important to her,' said the Queen Mother. 'Much of her time was spent keeping in touch with them, and she went abroad a lot visiting her friends and relatives. She read everything she could lay her hands on.'

The Queen Mother's own life has been filled to overflowing by some of these same things and many others besides. She has gone abroad a great deal both privately and on public service. She has read a wide variety of books ranging from P. G. Wodehouse to Ada Leverson ('The Sphinx').

OPPOSITE *HM Queen Elizabeth The Queen Mother at eighty. Her Majesty in the grounds of Royal Lodge, Windsor.*

LEFT *As Colonel-in-Chief of the Black Watch, the Queen Mother visited the 1st Battalion of the regiment as her first public engagement after the death of her husband.*

Wodehouse is such a favourite that she gallantly offered to fly to the USA and confer on him his knighthood. And she has collected pictures, listened to music, cultivated gardens (her own and others') and promoted the Sport of Queens. In this chapter we shall follow her around the globe and into the world of literature and the royal stud. If her family crop up on the way, this is only to be expected with a Queen Widow who is also a Queen Mother, Queen Grandmother and Queen Great-grandmother. Her widowhood is already twenty-eight years long, but there has never been a bare patch.

Never, that is to say, except in the first months.

Her first public engagement after the King's death was to bid farewell to her regiment, the Black Watch, on its departure for Korea in May 1952. She had had only three months in which to recover, and she wore the black that Hartnell had been forbidden to use during the blitz because it might have depressed people. She wore deep black for a full year. Now her black dress was matched by the Scots' black arm-bands; and in her speech she did not risk introducing her husband's name. Nevertheless her public composure appeared so impregnable that old Princess Marie Louise felt moved to tell Queen Elizabeth how brave she was. 'Not when I am alone,' said Queen Elizabeth.

And indeed, to those who knew the truth, it seemed doubtful at times whether the crushed Queen Mother would ever emerge again into the active world. Would she not retire completely, say to the remote Castle of Mey? While she was staying at Birkhall, her Household would try to coax her into inviting friends over who were visiting Balmoral. 'Oh, no, they won't want to come,' she would reply. Or even more sadly, 'No one understands . . .' No one understood that she had given up a 'human' life for a 'royal' life (in the best sense) and now both lives seemed to have come to an end.

Queen Elizabeth's later resilience was an act of will. She was helped, perhaps, by the irresistible Winston Churchill. When *he* was staying at Balmoral he did not wait for an invitation to Birkhall, but turned up uninvited. The beginning of Queen Elizabeth's emergence dates from this surprise visit. No one knows what he said to her. But it worked.

It was not till 1953 that the royal travels really began. The Queen Mother and Princess Margaret flew out by jet to Southern Rhodesia that summer for the centenary of Cecil Rhodes' birth. They landed at Salisbury, the first travellers to do so in a Comet. The airfield was still unfinished. Not that a Comet held any terrors for the intrepid Queen Mother. Sir Miles Thomas, then the Chairman of BOAC, recalls in his memoirs the day of a 'royal sprint' when the Queen Mother took the controls of a new Comet from the test-pilot, and flew the plane for a few minutes over Europe 'faster than a meteor' – in fact, until it began to porpoise. 'I still shudder every time I think of that flight,' wrote Thomas afterwards; for it was soon to be demonstrated that Comets could suffer from disastrous structural weakness. The Queen Mother, in writing to thank him for such a rapturous experience, added, 'What the passengers thought I really don't like to say!'

Queen Elizabeth's personal feelings for the black Africans were what would now be called 'paternalistic', though 'maternal' would be a better word. She loved them as a Queen Mother should. Once while she was addressing the Masai during a fearful drought the heavens opened, to shouts of 'Long live the Rain Goddess!'

Poor Princess Margaret had just begun the long two years' wait for Peter Townsend. She cannot have been the gayest of companions, and indeed she fell ill and had to miss part of the tour. But her mother's devotion to her knew no bounds, and travel always seemed a panacea. Major Harvey, Queen Elizabeth's former Treasurer, remembers how eager the Queen had been that Margaret should enjoy herself and see the world as a very young Princess. He himself had escorted her around Italy even at a time when there was a £50 limit on travel expenditure – and a Press hoping in vain to spot an extra penny.

In Rhodesia the Queen Mother had twin aims: to distract her daughter and to get back into the saddle herself. The latter entailed a programme from which any self-pity was sternly eradicated. Might the tour as planned be too strenuous? Not at all. The Queen Mother's first comment was, 'It's not very crowded.' Once in Rhodesia she met an unexpectedly wet and cold season. Yet she wore a pretty silk dress without a coat at the windy official opening of the Rhodes Exhibition. Her Household feared that she must have felt frozen. Not at all. 'I was perfectly all right.'

It is in fact one of Queen Elizabeth's rules never to admit to cold, fatigue or even a temperature. She will not have a thermometer near her – until she is literally too ill to prevent it. A rough wind is another of Queen Elizabeth's remedies. 'That will blow the germs away,' she says.

Home again, the Queen Mother took on her new duties as the senior Counsellor of State, while the Queen and Prince Philip were away for their world tour of 1953–4. Having so recently been 'Ambassador Royal' in South Africa, the Queen Mother now received foreign ambassadors on her daughter's behalf in Clarence House. At Buckingham Palace she stood for four hours conferring New Year's honours at six separate Investitures. She had previously acted for King George VI both during and after the war, and has done so since on many occasions for Queen Elizabeth II. The Queen Mother's Investitures have two things in common. She smiles all the while she is bestowing ribbons or stars; and she invariably runs over her time. This last is entirely due to the lively conversations on which she loves to embark. If a row of wheelchairs is lined up in the spacious corridor, waiting to be sent through the doors to the foot of the platform where Her Majesty will greet their occupants, it is no use the officials looking at their watches. Her Majesty's conversational arts and imagination always take flight at the sight of a wheelchair. And if time also flies – what matter?

Perhaps one reason is that she has done some of her public work from a wheelchair herself. In 1960 she cracked a small bone in her foot (the second foot injury within fifteen months) and a fortnight later launched the *Northern Star* at Newcastle-upon-Tyne from a wheelchair with her left foot in a surgical boot, and her right foot of course in an elegant shoe.

Following the short Rhodesian visit of 1953 came the mighty and prolonged effort, in 1954, of a visit to the United States and Canada. Dorothy Laird, whose book on the Queen Mother is the first authorized biographical study of Her Majesty, calls 1954 a 'turning-point'.

The idea of this journey originated in a memorial fund to King George VI, supported by President Eisenhower and organized by Lew Douglas, pre-war American ambassador in London. The fund was to be used for training young men and women from the Commonwealth in the United States. Would a member of the Royal Family receive this substantial cheque? None was available but the Queen Mother. Could she sally out alone?

Even if she braced herself for the ordeal, it did not seem at first that such a sacrifice would be worthwhile. The British ambassador in Washington had put out feelers and found no great enthusiasm for the royal visitor – 'a middle-aged lady and a widow at that'. The streets might be empty. No one would recognize her ...

Without being told precisely of the less than thrilling welcome expected, Queen Elizabeth had her suspicions. But she kept her own counsel. It was the kind of challenge to which she invariably rose.

She sailed in the *Queen Elizabeth*, the liner she had herself launched before the war. Her lady-in-waiting was Lady Jean Rankin, who, to date, has served Queen Elizabeth for thirty-three years. The ladies were in for surprises.

The tour began quietly enough in New York. It was quite true that nobody much seemed to have heard of her. The 'crowds' – if such they could be called – were orderly. There were two major functions to be attended over a ten-day programme: the conferring on Her Majesty of an honorary degree by Columbia University, and the presentation of the King George VI Memorial cheque at the English Speaking Union.

Gradually Jean Rankin realized that something was happening. Every time they opened the door to go out, a bigger crowd had gathered than the day before. Suddenly it all began to snowball. The happy, jostling crowds; the taxi drivers spotting her and shouting, 'That's "Ma Queen"!'; the television lights, the cameras, the fanfares at every function; the full newspaper coverage. She was news. She had taken off. She had taken the controls. She was flying 'faster than a meteor' as in that Comet over Europe the previous year, but this time in no danger of a crash. When the Queen Mother expressed a wish to see Saks, the fashionable New York store, everyone in Saks and on the pavement outside expressed a counter-wish to see *her*. She could not get near the famous displays of costume jewellery, for she herself was the greatest 'show case' of all. Up and down in the lift flew the royal party trying to find an empty floor where peace still reigned. They never did.

In Washington she stayed with the Eisenhowers, fulfilling more functions. After shaking hands with her, the notorious Senator Joseph McCarthy said: 'She's sharp.' She then moved to the British Embassy where 'a small party' for 2,000 was given in her honour. She returned to England having lost five pounds in weight; sometimes the tension and excitement of a floodlit banquet was so great that she could not eat. After one such experience her New York hosts, the Pierson Dixons, sustained her with a late-night dish of scrambled eggs on a tray by the fire.

But when it was all over, the solid gains were there to be counted. According to one story, the Mayor of Boston attributed the sudden ending of 'bussing' troubles in his city to the presence of Queen Elizabeth. 'This person from another world changed the whole atmosphere!'

'Unbelievable what a difference it's made to our work,' said Sir Roger Makins (now Lord Sherfield), the British ambassador; 'it all goes through much quicker and more smoothly.' The Americans in fact *wanted* to please, thanks to this sensational 'Queen Mom'. She was given many affectionate names, including 'Ma Queen' and 'Queen Mom', neither of which stuck. Fortunately on one of her many Canadian tours a reporter called her the 'Queen *Mum*' and this did stick.

As for her bewitching effect on the diplomatic world, this was neatly explained by Sir Evelyn Baring, High Commissioner of the Sudan. 'The most fascinating of women', he called her; 'not intellectual but remarkably clever and very feminine'.

In 1955 Queen Elizabeth accepted an honour which was to grow from a small seed into a spreading tree, and incidentally to offer her new worlds to conquer in the realms of academic life, literature and the arts. She became Chancellor of London University. 'It was the spark,' says Sir Martin Gilliat her Private Secretary, 'which set off this tumultuously varied way of life.' Why she accepted this post in a hitherto unknown field can only be guessed at. But there may be some significance in the fact

Her Majesty becomes Chancellor of London University. The inauguration, 1955.

Wearing one of her distinctive feathery hats the Queen Mother sits for a seventy-fifth birthday portrait at her London home, Clarence House.

that her young daughter Margaret was making her great renunciation this year. It would be characteristic of her mother to feel that she must do something for youth, whose tribulations, ideals and achievements she so well understood and felt for so deeply. (She would have liked to become Chancellor of Rhodesia University also, but unfortunately the declaration of UDI dashed her hopes.) As London University's first woman Chancellor she congratulated them at her installation – to cheers and laughter – on their advanced views.

Since that happy day in 1955, Queen Elizabeth has worked enthusiastically for London University in all its ramifications. One example of her activities must suffice. For a considerable period during the seventies, Chelsea College (a part of London University) negotiated to take over and develop the 'Marjon' site along the King's Road. This historic site, known as 'Marjon' because it was occupied by the former colleges of St Mark and St John, includes the fine eighteenth-century building called Stanley House. An earlier Stanley House had stood on the same site in Tudor times, where the Stanley family entertained Sir Walter Raleigh and perhaps also Shakespeare's players. Coincidentally, Queen Elizabeth's ancestor, Mary Eleanor, Countess of Strathmore, bought Stanley House in 1777, and from there made one of the many botanical collections for which Chelsea is still celebrated.

But it seemed that rival claimants to the site might 'gazump' Chelsea's offer, and, if successful, demolish the ancient buildings and park. Sir Martin Gilliat, Queen Elizabeth's Private Secretary, therefore, was instructed by Her Majesty to approach the Secretary of State for the Environment, Michael Heseltine:

... In the twenty-four years that she has held the appointment [he wrote] Queen Elizabeth has identified herself in a very personal way with the affairs of every College, Faculty and School, and it is in regard to the hopes of Chelsea College to acquire the 'Marjon' site that The Queen Mother feels a very special concern.

The long and intricate history of the negotiations is well known to Her Majesty, and Queen Elizabeth readily appreciates the complexities of the problem. Many representations have been made to the Queen Mother to help the College to acquire the facilities it so urgently needs and at the same time to ensure the preservation of an historic site.

Chelsea College has since triumphed, becoming once again (as it has been with one short break since 1843) the owner of the site.

I owe to Professor Ragnhild Hatton, Dean of the Faculty of Economics from 1974 to 1978, a vivid account of Queen Elizabeth's methods at degree givings. Up to the year 1975 Her Majesty had 'hooded' all graduates presented to her for degrees, both those who were 'bachelors', and those receiving higher degrees; a personal act that the students greatly appreciated. Then, with ever growing numbers, it was too tiring to 'hood' everybody, and she concentrated on the conferring of Honorary Degrees in the Senate House, on Foundation Day, where she remained seated throughout, after delivering her 'Charge', or speech, standing.

In the days when there were two receptions in the Senate House on Foundation Day going on at once in different rooms, some of the students would worry that she should not have time to meet them all, and would have to miss them out. But she never did. 'She was truly wonderful with the young, and gave the impression of having all the time in the world.'

The Presentation of Degrees – three a year in the Albert Hall, at two of which Her Majesty normally presided – is also always preceded by the Chancellor's 'Charge'. 'Queen Elizabeth hardly looked at her notes,' observed Professor Hatton. This was because she was so eager to establish contact with the students' families who were present in very large numbers in the Albert Hall. 'I always watched the parents' faces,' says Professor Hatton: 'Some were thrilled, others deeply moved.'

Queen Elizabeth reached the age of seventy-five in 1975. Before that year's Foundation Day dinner she looked at the list of previous Chancellors. 'I see thay all retire at seventy-five,' she said. 'I've enjoyed it so much.' A parting present was all ready for her. Then she got up. 'I've decided to carry on!' Jubilation. And Professor Hatton adds, 'One could *feel* her heartfelt enjoyment.' She retired at the end of 1980.

·The Albert Hall functions were a considerable test even though Her Majesty remained seated. They lasted some two-and-a-half hours with bursts of organ music and a seemingly endless snake of young men and women filing past, the Deans of their respective Faculties reading out name after name.

A religious service also takes place on Presentation Day each year, at St Paul's, Westminster Abbey or Westminster Cathedral. In 1976 it was held in the Abbey and a Lesson was read from the Book of Job, which would have appealed profoundly to Queen Elizabeth: 'Behold, the fear of the Lord, that is wisdom; and to depart from evil understanding.' In Queen Elizabeth's eyes, good understanding is indeed the highest understanding that any teacher or parent can impart.

Besides these great events, the Queen Chancellor welcomed the countless informal occasions when she could use her influence positively. She visited students at their centres of activity, carefully read all University reports, contributed money or gifts for raffles, gave advice on questions like new premises or changes in statutes, visited their boat clubs or dances or small parties. Finding herself at one most successful students' dance in the nervous arms of an inexperienced President, she congratulated him on not having knocked off her tiara – 'yet!' She presented annually at Malet Street on behalf of the Students' Union the testimonials to people they wished to honour. One year it was to a lady on the catering staff who had cut her millionth sandwich.

Academic 'wisdom' is also an essential part of 'good understanding', and in November 1972 Queen Elizabeth launched a grand appeal for a new building in which to house the British Library of Political and Economic Science, an integral part of the London School of Economics. Her written appeal emphasized that the LSE's 'priceless resources' in books and manuscripts must be readily available to scholars and men and women of affairs.

Among these treasures was a letter dated 1896 from Sidney Webb, rejoicing that the sum of £1,500 had been privately collected towards the first LSE library. Some eighty years later, in September 1978, the Queen Mother was congratulating the Appeal's Committee on having raised over £1,800,000 from private sources towards the new library. There is no doubt that her own hard work had ensured a generous response, especially where contributions from foreigners were hoped for. The Queen Mother's name acts like magic all over the world.

Finally came the day in July 1979 when Queen Elizabeth the Queen Mother rose to declare the new Library open. After congratulating all concerned, she let herself go in a moment of wit as well as wisdom, invoking the great name of John Ruskin, a pioneer in adult education:

Ruskin, in a lecture, once made the somewhat stern observation: 'What do we, as a nation, care about books? How much do you think we spend altogether on our libraries, public or private, as compared with what we spend on our *horses*?'

The rest of Her Majesty's remark was drowned in laughter, and that laugh of course depended on the whole audience knowing that the Royal Family is horse-mad. It is said that when Princess Anne and Mark Phillips announced their engagement, the Queen said happily: 'I shouldn't wonder if their children are four-legged.' Nor are the Queen herself and the Queen Mother above horse-worship.

It all began with a sparkling dinner-table conversation at Windsor in

OPPOSITE *Preceded by the former Master of the Horse, the Duke of Beaufort and other Knights of the Garter, Queen Elizabeth walks in procession to the annual Garter service at Windsor with Prince Charles.*

1949 between the Queen Consort (as she still was) and Lord Mildmay of Flete – a brilliant gentleman rider and breeder of steeplechasers. When 'Lordy' Mildmay suddenly began telling the Queen Consort how he had ridden 'blind' a horse called Cromwell in the Grand National because a slipped disc prevented him from moving his head, an answering spark awoke in her. Sensing her excitement he asked, 'Why not become an owner yourself, Ma'am?' 'Shall we?' the Queen asked Princess Elizabeth.

The shadow of the King's illness hung over both the Elizabeths, and each felt that this adventurous interest might take the other's mind off the impending tragedy. Together they bought Monaveen, an Irish nine-year-old, and raced him in Princess Elizabeth's colours. He won several races for them but the next year, 1950, had to be put down after he broke his leg at Hurst Park. This broke Princess Elizabeth's heart. She abandoned steeplechasing for flat racing and breeding.

1950 was a year of destiny for her mother. Poor 'Lordy' having been accidentally drowned in May, the Queen bought one of his best horses, Manicou, the half-brother of Cromwell. Although Cromwell is not the best name for a royal horse's relative, Manicou did the Queen proud.

The Queen was his sole owner. 'Mummy wouldn't share with *anybody* now,' Princess Margaret told Peter Cazalet, the Queen's trainer. She raced him in her own colours, the Strathmore pale blue, buff stripes, pale blue sleeves and black cap with gold tassel. He won at Kempton Park in November, the first time that a Queen's horse had won since Queen Anne's horse won in 1714 (it was Queen Anne who established Royal Ascot) and the first ever National Hunt win for a Queen. Manicou also sired The Rip, a favourite horse who shared with Laffy and Double Star the honour of winning for the Queen Mother her first racing hat-trick. The second came three years later, with Arch Point, Gay Record and Super Fox.

The wins mounted up swiftly, especially in the sixties when the Queen Mother had up to fifteen horses in training. She had soon won her hundredth race and today (1980) her score is well over 300. She pays for her horses out of her own money, never bets and is strictly non-commercial. Nevertheless, what began as a diversion has developed into devotion.

The effect of racing upon the Queen Mother is quite as worthy of study as the record of her successes. Why, for instance, does she stick to 'the sticks'? There is something in her temperament that responds. All the excitements of racing seem to be multiplied a hundred times when the hazards of fences and water are involved. Moreover, racing releases the royal personality for a moment from the thraldom of what is arranged, put on the agenda, laid on. No racing result is laid on. Anything can happen, and often does.

No doubt she felt it was a pity that her beloved grandson Charles was last past the post on Sea Swell at Sandown in March 1980, for his first ever 'chase, the Duke of Gloucester Memorial Trophy. But he delighted everybody by his 'winning' ways and comments. 'You've got to start somewhere,' he said, 'and I wasn't too far behind' – a mere 400 feet.

The case of Devon Loch is an example of the unscheduled climax. The Queen Mother's Devon Loch was within an ace of winning for her the 1956 Grand National when he suddenly pancaked, for no known reason. One could hear the commentator's jubilant voice abruptly change to a wail, while the crowd's cheers for a royal win sank into horrified silence; incidentally showing a visiting Russian, Malenkov, that the British really did want their 'Queen Mum' to win. Harold Nicolson was another visitor. 'The Queen Mother never turned a hair,' he recorded, but simply said, 'I must go down and comfort those poor people.' 'Please don't be upset,' she told Dick Francis the jockey and thriller writer; 'that's racing.' It was also, on the Queen Mother's part, 'the most perfect display of dignity' that Nicolson had ever seen.

A more down-to-earth tribute was paid to her by Peter Cazalet's Head Lad, Jim Fairgrieve (quoted by Frances Donaldson):

... Saturday morning, Her Majesty would be on the gallops watching the horses work. It was great to watch her in her wellington boots and headscarf, an icy wind blowing, sometimes a sleety shower. Her head would be up facing the gallop and enjoying every minute of it ...

The Queen Mother, famed for her involvement in the 'Sport of Kings', with her horse Devon Loch at Kempton Park in 1956.

ABOVE *With Prince
Charles and Princess
Anne at Ascot in 1979.*

RIGHT *Queen Elizabeth
The Queen Mother with
Princess Margaret at the
Badminton Horse Trials.*

LEFT *Her Majesty and Princess Margaret with the Queen's horse,* Valuation, *during Royal Ascot, 1978.*

BELOW *The Queen Mother congratulates jockey David Nicholson after he had won the Whitbread Gold Cup on* Mill House *at Sandown in April 1967.*

There can be little doubt that another attraction of the sport for her is the opportunity it provides to wear old clothes. Her Majesty welcomes the change from tiara to headscarf, from high heels to wellies. To be out in all weathers is not a hardship but heaven.

Her close friend and trainer, Peter Cazalet, died in 1973, and Fulke Walwyn has ably taken over. Sadly, the last Lingfield Races to which Cazalet could look forward in September 1972 were called off entirely owing to a persistent deluge from Friday to Sunday. Her Majesty as usual was staying at Fairlawne, the Cazalets' family home near Tonbridge where her horses were trained. On one of the wet afternoons of that weekend a house-guest happened to put her head disconsolately out of the window. There on the croquet lawn below was a little figure with a mallet, blue raincoat and blue sou'wester, manfully splashing through the puddles and just hitting one of the 'sticks' before Martin Gilliat did so. They were the wrong kind of 'sticks' but better than nothing.

Her qualities as a 'good sport' are well known, but there is always room for a new story. She would often visit Peter and Zara Cazalet for lunch at Fairlawne without the usual escort of lady-in-waiting, secretary, dresser and page. One day, arriving unexpectedly early at the stables, she was met by the Cazalets' twelve-year-old son Anthony, the proud possessor of a ramshackle filthy Ford Popular, which he was allowed to exercise on the mown rides. 'Ma'am, would you like me to drive you back to the house?' 'Of course. Such fun!' So Anthony bumped the Queen Mother not just back to the house but through the home woods, uphill and down dale, in and out of ruts and pot-holes and all around the estate, while she clung for dear life to the dash-board.

To her, Peter Cazalet was the much-loved 'Fuehrer'. She trusted his judgment absolutely, though she was not above twitting him now and then on some point of fact. 'What, haven't you read your *Sporting Life*? After his lamented death, she gave a present to every stable lad connected with her horses. She is considered the ideal owner, both for knowledge and enthusiasm. There is no blame for failure. 'Ma'am, the horse has hit itself in the box . . .' No one is to blame, not even the darling horse.

The same goes for her Household, or 'my little family', as she prefers to call them. 'Ma'am, I've left your speech behind . . .' They were on a plane, and another speech had to be hurriedly constructed. After the new speech had been successfully delivered, she said: 'I think we did that rather nicely, didn't we?' It was not a royal 'we' but a co-operative one. Part of her personal gift has always been to draw people into her immediate circle, and make them feel for the moment like intimate collaborators.

From 1954 onwards, Queen Elizabeth's official travels around the globe have continued at a smart trot: the United States of America; France twice; the Federation of Rhodesia and Nyasaland twice; Australia, New Zealand, Fiji twice; Kenya, Uganda; Italy; Gibraltar, Tunisia, Sardinia; Northern Ireland three times; Denmark; Iran, Cyprus, Channel Islands, Holland; West Germany (to visit the British Army of the Rhine); and Canada eight times.

In 1958 Queen Elizabeth became the first royalty to do a 'round-the-world' flight. It was incredibly strenuous: in Australia there were some days with nothing between her and a fierce sun but her white parasol with its green lining; other days with sheets of torrential rain. But she never cut anything from her programme. And she even extended her labours by insisting on 'talk-abouts' among the people, a procedure that she and George VI had spontaneously initiated in Canada some twenty years before, and which has now been developed into 'walk-abouts' and expanded by her daughter Elizabeth II.

Every time they returned from an engagement in Australia, Lady Jean Rankin remembers, 'the whole place would be *heaped* with flowers'. Garden parties became a test of strength for the staff. The Queen Mother's escort would link arms and dig their heels into the grass. 'But I've come a thousand miles to see her!' some anguished voice would protest. The patient reply would be, 'You won't see her by laying her out'. On one Australian airstrip the wind, of hurricane force, blew the white cock's feathers clean out of the Governor's hat; they were replanted by his ADC. Even the royal car sometimes behaved like a

In 1958, Queen Elizabeth The Queen Mother visited Australia. 'I've come a 1,000 miles to see her,' protested one onlooker afraid of missing the opportunity.

minor tornado. In Tasmania their driver was told to slow down for a road-side crowd. He stopped so suddenly that Her Majesty and Lady Jean both landed on the floor. (The same thing once happened in England, with an energetic chauffeur rightly called Mr Hurl.)

The Queen Mother's conveyances showed themselves accident-prone. In 1928 a fire on board her ship: in 1958 three Super-Constellation breakdowns. The first of those was particularly unpleasant for Lady Jean Rankin, since she was an experienced pilot herself and could hear that something had gone disastrously wrong with one of the engines. She looked out and saw that it had packed up, its propellor all askew. Through all the delays Queen Elizabeth maintained her fabulous patience and good humour, even at Mauritius where the royal party sat dripping for three days with nothing to do. She seemed more sorry for the pilots and engineers than for herself. Her Majesty arrived home at last several days late and reduced to wearing a tweed coat with white shoes.

It was also this most exhausting tour that convinced Jean Rankin that there was everything to be said for the Royal Yacht. Without it, life could be a nightmare. Never in one place for more than a night or two, the staff were continually packing and unpacking. One came back to the hotel dead beat at 1.00 a.m., to be woken again by the rustling of tissue paper at 4.00. All day long the Queen Mother was being asked to decide in advance what she would wear there ... or there ... or there. She might have to change half-a-dozen times in one day, with no chance for her famous impulsiveness, spontaneity or inspiration. Whereas on the Royal Yacht everything was *there*. In an emergency a Royal Yacht would justify its expense by becoming a hospital ship. Without a Royal Yacht the Royal Family were liable to become hospital cases themselves.

Altogether Queen Elizabeth has made twenty-seven official visits abroad and six private ones between 1960 and 1980.

All the private visits have been to France. They have gradually grown into an annual holiday. France was an obvious Mecca for the Queen Mother. The country is gay and beautiful in just the ways she most appreciates, she is an accomplished French speaker, and Anglo-French relations can always do with an unofficial polishing.

The first holiday visit sprang from a chance conversation with Sir Pierson Dixon nearly twenty years ago, when he was British Ambassador in Paris. 'Why don't you come to France?' he asked Queen Elizabeth. Why not? So Her Majesty took one floor of a French hotel, and with a party of English friends visited the châteaux of the Loire. A distinguished Frenchman, the Viscomte de Noailles, took charge. After the Loire Valley, she rented in 1965 a little fifteenth-century house in Provence and from there explored the surrounding country, châteaux, Provençal customs. One of her friends remembers a tour of Burgundy:

This charming little figure in blue – *everybody* falls for her. They may be alarmed at first – after all, a Queen of England! – but they fall for her in a minute. In Burgundy (1976) she met all sorts of people, most of them not formally introduced. A *sous-préfet's* wife gave her a tiny brown paper parcel – a mouth-organ. She blew a merry tune on it and put it in her handbag – kept it for months.

The Duchess of Magenta was her hostess and a Canon of Autun was there for dinner – no one introduced him but the next day he showed her his Cathedral, the choir-boys holding pink roses and singing Purcell in her honour.

On the third night a choir came from Beaune and sang Burgundian songs. At the end of the evening she went up to her room and the choir went on singing from across the moat. So she played on her mouth-organ out of the window – and then the son-in-law of the house replied again, on the French horn.

During a visit to one of the beautiful churches I overheard a Frenchman talking to his wife and saying '*Mais elle n'est pas fière.*'

No, she is not proud. To the French she is a heroine. A passionate sight-seer, she will visit churches, châteaux, vineyards intensively for four days on end. She has made speeches in French in the Rothschild country

ABOVE *The Queen Mother takes her place in the royal box at Covent Garden for a 1963 performance of* The Marriage of Figaro.

RIGHT *Helping Ben Travers to celebrate his ninety-third birthday on the stage of a London theatre.*

(unofficial) and at the Sorbonne (official) before opening the new British Institute.

In 1966 it looked for a moment as if even Queen Elizabeth's amazing vitality was to take a knock, when she underwent a serious operation. But even in her worst moments her wit bubbled up. In thanking one of her doctors for his bulletin she added, 'of course the word "comfortable" has a different meaning to the surgeon than to the patient.' The first time she reappeared next year on the receiving line at a Buckingham Palace party she looked small and wan. When guests congratulated her with heartfelt pleasure on her recovery, she thanked them with touching fervour, as though surprised that she had been missed. Later that year, in July, she paid an official visit to the Atlantic Provinces of Canada, based on HMS *Britannia*.

Someone at home remembered that she had been demonstrating the hula-hula on her way back from Honolulu four months before her operation; and she has been dancing again at small parties in London and at Royal Lodge ever since. It is the pastime that Queen Elizabeth, a Scot, most enjoys. She has a marvellous capacity for getting friends to dance after dinner when all they have thought themselves up to was conversation or a quiet parlour game. Quite recently, at Royal Lodge, she conjured Lord Hailsham into throwing away his sticks and joining the party in a Welsh jig. 'But it was a *miracle*, my dear Quintin!' said a friend afterwards. 'Yes, but a short-lived one,' replied Lord Hailsham sadly; for once out of the magical presence he was back with his sticks.

Another friend, the late Tom Goff, the harpsichord expert who was descended from Mrs Jordan the actress – mother of William IV's ten children – and proud of it, used to give a small dinner for the Queen Mother once a year in his Chelsea house. 'There was music and then we danced,' says Lord David Cecil, who was there; 'none of us was young, but there we were, dancing...'

David Cecil has been a frequent visitor over the years at the King's Lynn Festival. These are the occasions when Queen Elizabeth's sense of fun and her devotion to the arts come together under the inspiration of the Festival's organizer, Ruth Lady Fermoy.

Queen Elizabeth comes of a musical family [Lord David says]. She herself loves music. She has a very retentive memory and can play and sing for you any of the old music-hall songs you ask. Her sister Rose was a talented amateur pianist. During the Lynn Festival, Queen Elizabeth would invite musicians and artists like Benjamin Britten or Noël Coward back to Sandringham afterwards, to play and sing favourite pieces and songs.

Sandringham is extraordinarily comfortable, despite its huge Edwardian bedrooms, still full of the original furniture – sturdily philistine, with flamboyant screens, portraits, fabergé ornaments.

While the Festival is running Queen Elizabeth comes down every morning at about 11 a.m. The horses are visited. She finds time to show her guests interesting sights in the neighbourhood, such as Wyndham Ketton-Kremer's beautiful house, or a church. One day it may be a picnic on Lord Leicester's beach at Holkham. Those who want to can bathe. The Queen Mother always

Her Majesty dances with Major Alan Ferrier at a royal Silver Jubilee ball in Scotland, 1977.

does the unpacking. After lunch she goes for a little walk by herself, with her dogs. It is rather touching.

It was the Sitwells and their circle who during the war were mainly responsible for Queen Elizabeth's conversion from the agreeable amateurism of her background to serious concern for and understanding of the arts. It was Queen Elizabeth's idea in 1941, when Windsor Castle was threatened by bombs, to preserve at least its portrait in a series of water-colours by John Piper. She persuaded the King to commission them. When the Castle survived the blitz, she said with satisfaction: 'We still have the Pipers, *and* the Castle.'

Years later, Sir John Betjeman the Poet Laureate would find himself reading poetry aloud after dinner at Royal Lodge. The widow of Paul Nash the painter owes her Civil List pension to the Queen Mother's influence; and also the pension's increase, when Her Majesty discovered, on enquiry, that inflation had made the original pension inadequate.

Sir Rupert Hart-Davis, author and man of letters, has given a very human impression of the Queen Mother presenting the Duff Cooper Memorial Prize for literature to Lawrence Durrell in 1957:

> The Queen Mother looked quite lovely in silver ... I explained the simple drill to her, and she was wide-eyed as a little girl who had never done such a thing before. After Durrell had been presented and they had taken up their position, she whispered to him: 'I'm terrified. Aren't you?' which did much to calm his palpable fright ...

How does Queen Elizabeth compare with other royalties as a patron of the arts? Queen Victoria, after the death of the Prince Consort in 1861, bought and commissioned many pictures and works of art; but neither she nor King Edward VII showed any interest in the best of contemporary British or foreign painting. Edward VII and Queen Alexandra never bought a good picture and, in their enthusiasm to pull down so much of what Victoria and Albert had built up, they destroyed many pretty and colourful schemes of interior decoration at Buckingham Palace and replaced them by monotonous variations in gold and white.

Queen Mary was a devoted custodian of the Royal Collections, but there is no evidence that she was attracted to the more important, or the most beautiful movements in contemporary art.

By contrast, Queen Elizabeth has an instinctive love of pictures and a delight in the beauty of paint for its own sake, as well as an affectionate sympathy with pictures of a family and sporting nature. And she has a wonderful collection of china at Clarence House, especially Chelsea china given her for her birthday each year by her husband.

In a sense Queen Elizabeth's ideas on collecting may be regarded as 'old-fashioned' but none the less in line with many people's feelings today. She does not believe in pictures getting into public galleries which could remain in the houses where they began. She would not have agreed with Queen Mary, who let slip two opportunities to obtain for the Royal Collection a family portrait which eventually ended up in the National Gallery.

The Queen Mother's study at Royal Lodge, Windsor.

Queen Elizabeth's intense belief in the family – not only *her* family but *your* family, *all* families – has led her to salvage many Bowes-Lyon possessions from the auction rooms, using them to beautify one or other of her homes. She was shocked to learn that the pen with which Edward VIII signed the Abdication had been sold. Clarence House is adorned with contemporary portraits of George III's family framed in plaster scroll-work; though only the first floor of this eighteenth-century mansion still retains its original Nash ceilings and tall mahogany doors.

Fine modern paintings have also been collected by Queen Elizabeth, above all *The Rock* by Monet and Sisley's *The Seine near St Cloud*; while English painters are represented by, among others, Augustus John, L.S.

Lowry, Duncan Grant, Paul Nash, Matthew Smith, Sir William Nicholson and Dame Ethel Walker. From Australia have come Nolan's *Strange Fruit* and Drysdale's *Man in a Landscape*. A sketch of the 12th Earl of Strathmore by Herring, mounted and wearing the Strathmore racing colours, has an obvious place. Dr Roy Strong, Director of the Victoria and Albert Museum, once complained that the Royal Family rarely made a bow to modern portraiture. Queen Elizabeth is an exception, as the stimulating portraits of herself by Graham Sutherland and Augustus John testify. Her cleverness comes out in Sutherland's picture as nowhere else, and her sparkling 'Titania' quality in John's. On her eightieth birthday Dr Strong said: 'She has a genuine and abiding interest in the arts of her generation, like the beautiful boxes Oliver Messel made for her, the art of Cecil Beaton and of course Rex Whistler. Her interest is less patronage than a real feeling for things.'

Whether she herself is easy or hard to paint remains a matter for dispute. The knowledgeable biographer Godfrey Thomas calls her 'a favourite of the portrait painters'. Helen Cathcart, however, another royal biographer, describes her as 'the despair of artists'. One thing is certain: Queen Elizabeth deeply appreciates the whole ambience of modern painting. 'Don't you love visiting studios?' she asks. 'The whole thing is so fascinating and such fun.'

Her devoted Household and friends have contributed various *objets d'art* to Her Majesty's personal collection. Martin Charteris, the Queen's former Private Secretary, designed and cast in bronze a splendid dummy fireback for the dining-room at the Castle of Mey. As a farewell present, Major Tom Harvey of her Household commissioned Lawrence Whistler to make for her desk a gilt and crystal triptych, the central panel holding each day's list of engagements. Besides pictorial engraving, Whistler composed some verses for the side panels: 'Pleasures' to the left, 'Duties' to the right. Since Queen Elizabeth is a royal patron 300 times over, her list of engagements is never less than crammed.

But alas, her 'Indian Summer' has not been an unbroken string of pleasures and pleasurable duties – for the Queen Mother finds all her duties pleasant. Sorrows and ordeals have also come her way.

In 1976 Princess Margaret and Lord Snowdon were legally separated, and divorced two years later. It was a bitter blow to the Queen Mother, who had passionately hoped for her daughter's happiness at last, and had optimistically called the high-spirited young couple 'two of a kind'. But there is an old adage, 'Two of a kind never agree.' Neither was prepared to relinquish their own perfectly reasonable ambitions in favour of the other, while Lord Snowdon was not cut out from the start to walk the step behind his wife that protocol demanded.

Peter Townsend would have done it from habit and training; Prince Philip does it from conviction and love. Lord Snowdon's artistic career could not ultimately benefit from too close a connection with the Establishment. A comparison between the school reports of Philip Mountbatten and Tony Armstrong-Jones points the discrepancy. Philip was head boy of Gordonstoun, with the 'greatest sense of service' and a

trophy for the best all-rounder in the school. Of Tony his prep school headmaster wrote: 'Armstrong-Jones may be good at something, but it's nothing we teach here.'

One particular studio portrait that Lord Snowdon made of his wife in 1967 (reproduced in his fascinating *Personal View*, 1979) shows how clearly he soon realized the sad truth. As a quite young girl, Chips Channon had sensed in her 'a Marie Antoinette aroma'. Snowdon's photograph shows the same poignant beauty.

Nevertheless, there is no reason why happiness should not supervene for the warm and spontaneous Princess Margaret as well as Lord Snowdon. (He is now married to Lucy Lindsay-Hogg, and they have a daughter, Frances.) Nor is it self-evident that the 'royal system' is at fault, as the historian Paul Johnson suggests in an otherwise sympathetic article. Quoting Queen Elizabeth I's saying, 'I know what it is to be the Second Person', Johnson appears to believe that there is no real niche for younger sisters, and presumably younger brothers, in the royal system:

Princess Margaret [he writes] should be seen as to some extent the victim of a royal system which is essentially heartless and which never knows when or how far to modernize itself.

But who does know exactly when or how far to modernize? Does the Church know? Or Parliament? Or do parents know exactly? No doubt the system, like all systems, sometimes lags. And a Press that is often insensitive and unfair to Princess Margaret does not help. Nevertheless, what is basically wrong with 'second persons'? The world is full of them in all walks of life, and there seems no reason why Princess Margaret, like so many other 'seconds', should not in time find her 'identity'; nor that if Prince Charles has two daughters, the second is bound to be unlucky.

The horrible assassination of Lord Mountbatten, the Dowager Lady Brabourne and two young boys, one his grandson, brought stark tragedy into the Queen Mother's eightieth year. The blow to her beloved grandson, Prince Charles, was particularly severe. 'I adored him and miss him so dreadfully now,' he said at his great-uncle's memorial service.

Apart from the grief of personal losses, including that of her youngest brother David, Queen Elizabeth had to face a considerable ordeal in 1972. The Duke of Windsor died and his widow came to Windsor for the funeral. The Queen Mother was gentle with her, as became a Queen, taking the sadly bemused woman by the arm. But with the two royal brothers now dead, Queen Elizabeth would have been less than human if she had not remembered that one widow had enjoyed her husband's companionship for thirty-five years, and the other widow – herself – for only twenty-nine; though she and Bertie had married fourteen years before Edward. At the same time she may have wondered whether that long twenty years' exile of the Windsors after her husband's death was right or necessary. While King George VI was alive, battling with the war, battling with ill-health, the added intractable problem of the Windsors would have been unthinkable. But there were twenty years between 1952 when King George VI died and 1972 when his brother Edward followed

Royal Wedding, 1973. The Queen Mother surrounded by her family at Buckingham Palace following the wedding of Princess Anne and Captain Mark Phillips.

him. One can only guess that it was a protracted interior struggle for Queen Elizabeth, most generous of human beings, between forgiving generosity towards the undeserving Windsors and loyalty to the memory of the long-suffering King. If loyalty won, it was because her feelings were not atrophied by age, despite her own dictum. 'The only regret one has as one grows older is that things do not matter so strongly.'

There have been, none the less, many latter-day events to bring Queen Elizabeth unbounded joy, and one of these was the 'silver' anniversary of

the Queen's marriage in the same year, 1972. Immediately in front of the Queen, Prince Philip and the Prince of Wales in their State landau, came the carriage procession of Queen Elizabeth The Queen Mother, rolling through London to St Paul's. There she sat in her carriage, with her two handsome grandsons opposite, Prince Andrew and Prince Edward. The Canon in Residence at St Paul's read the Second Lesson: 'And the rain descended, and the floods came, and the winds blew, and beat upon that house; and it fell not; for it was founded upon a rock.'

Eighty Years

9

B ECAUSE SHE is so nice ... That was the reason given by a Commonwealth country for wanting a visit from the Queen Mother. Admittedly there were other reasons: opening this, planting that, commemorating the other. But the over-riding one was simply, 'because she is so nice'.

When people know you are writing about her, unsolicited examples of her niceness pour in. One story concerns the opening of a new college chapel. The local bishop stumbled and might have fallen had she not quietly caught his arm and steadied him. Another is about a couple who lived in a cottage at the gates of Royal Lodge, and were bombed during the war. A friend visited them, expecting to find them very depressed.

But I found them in wonderful spirits [she writes], the wife telling me she was wearing one of the Queen's dresses, with handbag, and her husband one of the King's suits. What a simple yet wonderful way for the Queen to have given happiness and relief to these people, so typical really of her whole life.

The smiles she bestows upon way-out youth have sometimes been described as 'a trick'. 'She can't like them.' But she does. And she knows that smiles win more response than scowls.

Harold Nicolson marvelled at 'the horrible objects' in woodwork and pottery which she received with smiles from the students of Morley College. They did not look horrible to her, any more than did the two pottery dishes that Prince Andrew made for her 75th birthday.

If someone condoles with her on a boring event or tiresome person Queen Elizabeth says, 'Oh, but I found such and such a thing about them so interesting.' Her philosophy is to get *something* out of every experience. Nothing is to be wasted or fruitless. Nor are there any outcasts. Someone she has once liked is still liked, whatever happens.

It is sometimes said that her mesmeric effect on a crowd is due to her selecting one face and speaking to it, so that the individual in question is thrilled at being selected and communicates his pleasure. The truth, however, is that, whereas most speakers avoid the eyes in front of them and vaguely address a sea of faces, she has a gift for appearing to speak to every member of the audience.

She keeps no one at arm's length. In talking with reporters, she will always say 'my grandson' rather than Prince Charles or Prince Andrew; for many of us have grandsons but few are at home with princes. She enters into children's feelings. When, after meeting her, a child said,

OPPOSITE *Her Majesty's eightieth birthday, 4 August 1980. The Queen Mother accepts gifts from children outside Clarence House.*

'Ma'am, I've also met your daughter. Do you know she's the Queen?' Her Majesty replied, 'Yes, isn't it exciting?'

James Barrie, her family's neighbour in Scotland, defined charm in his play *What Every Woman Knows*: 'Oh, it's – it's a sort of bloom on women. If you have it, you don't need to have anything else; and if you don't have it, it doesn't much matter what else you have.' Every woman knows that this is the Queen Mother exactly. Asked to describe her charm in just a few words, one close friend immediately replied 'Instant sunshine'.

Charm, however, must not be sugary. 'The Queen Mother has a sense of humour as well,' says one of her friends, Woodrow Wyatt. 'Humour has a spice in it,' I point out. 'Yes,' says Wyatt, 'and she is not all sugar. She can be a little acid when necessary.'

Another ingredient of Queen Elizabeth's charm is her strength. Frances Donaldson has noticed that she is so strong she never needs to assert herself. 'She has such a reassuring manner you feel she has total control for both, and will never let you put a foot wrong.' David Cecil says: 'For someone so unaggressive she has a very strong personality.... She *could* be formidable.' He adds, 'I have never seen it.'

Queen Elizabeth's strength shows also in her signature. It is extraordinarily like the Queen's signature, each being upright and firm. But her daughter's is more rounded, while the mother's has a sharp point or two that seem to indicate the necessary touch of steel in a life where all has not been roses.

Her astonishing self-control is another aspect of her strength. No one has ever heard her lose her temper. Not once has she rebuked her daughters in front of the Household. At the same time she has the effect

OPPOSITE *The Queen Mother driving from Buckingham Palace in an open carriage on her way to the annual ceremony of Trooping the Colour.*

ABOVE *Watched by their parents, the Queen Mother's great-grandson, Peter Phillips, and great-nephew, the Earl of Ulster, join members of the Royal Family on the Palace balcony after Trooping the Colour, 1980.*

of liberating other people, of making them conscious of themselves in a way they were not before.

Her staff agree that she is 'generous and forgiving' to a fault. Like her mother, Lady Strathmore, she will treat a peccadillo with nothing worse than, 'Oh, dear.' She assumes complete loyalty (a favourite word) in others, and always resists the temptation to play 'The King card'. ('The King would never have allowed this or that.') The only exception was when she hoped that Princess Margaret's tour of the Seychelles would be abandoned while Archbishop Makarios was imprisoned there. But this was due to her especially protective feeling towards her daughter.

Her staff is small and efficient: only two permanent secretaries – and one extra for the 80th birthday year. 'Small is beautiful' could be one of her mottoes.

While I was talking to Sir Martin Gilliat in his office, the telephone constantly rang with requests for Her Majesty's presence over a year ahead. 'Put it in writing,' she always says, 'then we can concentrate our minds.' Though by temperament she likes to run things close, she is never actually late for an engagement she has accepted.

All her staff are helpful, courteous and smiling – down to the footman who let her corgis Blackie and Geordie out of Clarence House just as my car drew up to deliver a manuscript. One of them promptly darted underneath the car and prepared to dig in. 'Do you mind not moving until I get the dog out?' the footman asked smiling. He was tall and the car was low on the ground. It looked for a moment as if Her Majesty herself might have to be called to extricate her corgi, much as she had coaxed that terrier from a bomb-hole in the war. Fortunately the corgi surrendered first.

Her Household has organized many unusual events and no doubt will continue to do so in the eighties. Queen Elizabeth, for instance, is the first honorary lady member of the Press Club whose new building in Shoe Lane she opened in 1974. As there were fewer women present than men, she insisted on meeting every one of the women individually. In the last month of her eightieth birthday year they gave her a party at the Press Club. She played snooker – snooker not snooper. For though Queen Elizabeth gets on better with the Press than any of the Royal Family, she was as indignant as anyone at the harrying of Lady Diana Spencer and the snooping into an assignation with Prince Charles on the royal train, which in fact never happened.

In 1979 she was the first woman to become Lord Warden of the Cinque Ports. She expressed her pleasure at following two such great men as Sir Winston Churchill and Sir Robert Menzies 'in this ancient office'. It was a blustery day, worthy of a Britannia who rides the waves. She came on deck at 10.00 a.m. and was not in bed till long after midnight. Judges clung to their wigs, ladies to their hats. At the swooping fly-past an admiral flinched, but not Britannia. From Dover harbour to Dover streets, the little bright blue figure in high heels met the wind and met the people, finishing up with a reception for the notabilities of Kent.

Her stalwartness in rough weather comes from her being at heart a

OPPOSITE *'This ancient office.' Her Majesty in Rye, the first woman to hold office as Lord Warden of the Cinque Ports. 1980.*

The Queen Mother chats with a crowd that has waited patiently for a glimpse of their royal visitor.

countrywoman. It is not for nothing that she has been President of the Royal Horticultural Society, is President of the National Trust and has helped bring the country to town by patronizing the London Gardens Society. She expresses her addiction to country sports with characteristic humour. The gillie who goes with her salmon-fishing is called Mr Pearl. 'I just go to please Pearl,' she says with a mischievous laugh.

Queen Elizabeth has a strong sense of pleasure. Life is very much worth living. She has brought this *joie de vivre* into a Royal Family which ever since Albert the Prince Consort has shown a strain of self-doubt, as in George V and Queen Mary, laced with the self-indulgence of Edward VII. Edward VIII had both. *Joie de vivre* is an expression of selfless happiness.

No gathering at which Queen Elizabeth appears can be unaware of her alertness, vitality and life-giving grace. While signing the Visitors' Book after opening the Sue Ryder Foundation's Museum at Cavendish in 1979, the table collapsed; but Queen Elizabeth deftly caught the book in mid air and finished with a flourish. On a particularly wet July day that same year she arrived at a friend's for lunch wearing a lovely print dress covered with summer flowers and piped in apple green – with a hat to match. She looked like a piece of her own Chelsea china. 'At least, Ma'am, you've brought the summer on your dress,' said a guest. 'Isn't it awful? One simply doesn't know what to wear,' replied Her Majesty, charmingly implying that we all share exactly the same problems. From

garden flowers to the Physic Garden in Royal Hospital Road. 'Isn't it perfectly delicious?' she said, '– such fun.' Again two favourite words.

Her *joie de vivre* makes her a special favourite with the whole theatrical world: ballet, opera, drama, variety, the cinema and television. She was a brilliant performer in the television series, *Royal Heritage*. Moreover, she is an excellent mimic, once 'opening' a Sussex cottage that Lord Snowdon had acquired with a mock ceremony parodying herself.

How do these gifts, so sparkling and varied, contribute to the Monarchy?

Lord David Cecil picks out her two guiding lights as duty and patriotism. 'She has an innate sense of duty, which was greatly enhanced by the King. And she is very very patriotic. "I do like it," she will say, "I think it's so English."' David Cecil goes on to link her dramatic powers with her duty as a Queen. They are part of a unique 'performance'. (I put the word 'performance' in inverted commas because David Cecil rightly insists that the Queen Mother's splendid act is in no sense artificial or laid on.)

Her sense of duty and patriotism [he says] are helped by her dramatic sense. She thinks she *ought to* wave and give pleasure. And she is able to perform these feelings to the public. Others might have the gift, but suffer from the wrong friends – dreary advisers – while this gift can make some people unreliable, like Edward VIII.

With Queen Elizabeth The Queen Mother the gift is perfectly integrated with her sense of duty. Put another way, she is aware of her public position but the private person is not obliterated.

Hers is an honourable and simple view of life [continues David Cecil]. She has been able to put it across to the millions because of this gift of performance.

It is obvious that someone with this strong, uncomplicated view of life plus this 'gift of performance' will greatly influence what is called the 'mystique of Monarchy'. Today there is a tendency to downgrade the mystique. Harold Nicolson, author of the official life of George V, said: 'I fear I have no mystic feeling about the Monarchy.' Indeed he would laughingly have preferred for reward a dozen bottles of champagne or a travelling clock to 'that beastly KCVO'.

Queen Elizabeth's achievement has been to let in daylight on the 'mystique' without shattering its potency. She is probably more forthright in this respect than anyone else in her circle. There is the familiar story of her watching television at home with friends when the National Anthem suddenly struck up. 'Switch it off,' she exclaimed. 'Unless one is there it's embarrassing – like hearing the Lord's Prayer while playing canasta.'

A guest once arrived monstrously late for dinner at Fairlawne, the Cazalets' home, having completely lost the way. Her Majesty was kept waiting a long time for her dinner and no apologies could be too profuse. She accepted them with a beaming smile and the remark, 'It was lovely. For once I could watch the whole of Dad's Army.'

Way back in the fifties she had said rather bitterly, 'We – the Royal Family – are not supposed to be human.' Today that is all over. They *are* supposed to be human; but royal as well – not always the easiest combination. Queen Elizabeth has achieved the balance in many appealing ways. Her refusal to be rushed; her occasional changes of mind and indecisiveness (she once sent for the Koh-i-Noor diamond from the Tower to wear at a banquet and then, after it had arrived under elaborate escort, decided to wear something else); her temptation to spend a pound where a penny would do, after studying some alluring catalogue of flowers, pictures, books or antiques; all these things make her human.

The central theme of the Queen Mother's eightieth birthday celebrations was thanksgiving – for a Queen and for a very special person. A thanksgiving service was held at St Paul's Cathedral on 15 July. It was forty-eight hours since the sun had shone, so its fitful shining seemed true 'Queen's weather'. Outside the crowds were four-deep on the pavements and cameramen were clinging to Queen Anne's statue. Inside the vast cathedral (it held 2,700 people) the lighting varied dramatically from crystal chandeliers to television glare, from glittering mosaics to cool haunted aisles. A long golden banner covered a pillar opposite the pulpit, reiterating the thought of a great mystic, Julian of Norwich: 'All is well.' Into this splendour marched the first processions; ecclesiastics, City dignitaries, yeomen. A band played in the transept. Meanwhile the Queen Mother was on her way, Prince Charles at her side and honoured by a royal escort of Household Cavalry, hitherto accorded only to a reigning sovereign. The violet-blue of her hat and dress contrasted marvellously with the crimson cushions of her State landau and the scarlet uniforms. As she reached St Paul's and stood on the steps waving to the people, her feathers and the floating panels of her chiffon dress blew out in the stiff cool breeze. Onlookers wore coats, but not she.

A fanfare of silver trumpets heralded the procession of the Royal Family up the nave, between pyramids of pale pink and deep rose flowers, to their seats under the dome. The service was ecumenical, conducted by the Dean of St Paul's with the Moderator of the Church of Scotland reading the lesson, and Cardinal Hume saying two prayers. Dr Runcie the Archbishop of Canterbury gave the address: 'It is very difficult to fall in love with committees or policies, but the Queen Mother has shown a human face ... Royalty puts a human face on the operations of government' – which the press, in reporting, neatly adjusted to 'The Queen Mother has shown the human face of Royalty'. When Dr Runcie reminded us of the late King and his Queen in the East End during the war, the listening Queen Mother had tears in her eyes.

'A tribute from her childhood home' was the theme of the celebrations at St Paul's Walden Bury and Whitwell. They included an open day in the gardens of her old home, a lakeside concert, a fashion display where she was seen enjoying a green lolly, and in All Saints Church a photographic exhibition and festival of flowers. Returning to London the flower motif was repeated in St James's Park where a rose walk was planted in her honour. Exhibitions of photographs were held in

OPPOSITE *An eightieth birthday portrait of Her Majesty. The Queen Mother wears a gold and cream lace dress and, securing the Riband of the Garter, a small diamond brooch which Queen Victoria used for the same purpose.*

RIGHT *Queen Elizabeth arrives for one of the many gala occasions held in her honour during 1980.*

BELOW *The Queen Mother with the Prince of Wales drives to St Paul's in the 1902 State Landau for the Thanksgiving Service for Her Majesty's eightieth birthday.*

LEFT *The Queen Mother with her daughters, HM The Queen and HRH The Princess Margaret at Royal Lodge, Windsor.*

BELOW *Seated beneath the Cathedral's dome, the Queen Mother turns to smile at members of her family.*

ABOVE *A witty contrast by royal photographer Cecil Beaton, 1939. Queen Elizabeth sits between two temple caryatids in her Buckingham Palace garden.*

OPPOSITE *HM Queen Elizabeth The Queen Mother photographed in her garden by Norman Parkinson.*

Westminster Abbey and in the National Portrait Gallery, where her wedding dress was also displayed – a demure little affair compared with the shimmering crinolines of her reign and today's billowing chiffon. The official birthday photographs were taken by Norman Parkinson. He was immensely impressed by the vigour of Queen Elizabeth's health compared with five years before and by her eagerness to give him all possible help, even getting up early to discover a 'bower' in the gardens which might make an original setting.

On 17 July a garden party was held in Queen Elizabeth's honour at Buckingham Palace, which afforded those invited an opportunity to visit the settings of Cecil Beaton's earlier photographic masterpieces. Gleaming on the emerald lawn towards Hyde Park Corner entrance, stood the gigantic urn where she had once twirled her parasol; and in a temple nearby reared up those monstrous male caryatids whose arrogance emphasized her bewitching feminine charm.

And so dawned the birthday itself, Monday 4 August 1980. For days huge sacks of mail had been pouring into Clarence House. Eight more sackfuls were delivered early on the 4th. The first birthday present to arrive was a bouquet of eighty red roses from the Members of the Royal Philharmonic Orchestra, of which the Queen Mother is Patron. During the day two tributes came from her University of London, underlining her doubly gifted temperament. Lord Annan the Vice-Chancellor told the BBC that she possessed a sixth sense about what ought to be done; and a student said, 'We all love her because she is such a happy person.' In the morning papers appeared Sir John Betjeman's lines to her:

> ... Waves of goodwill
> Go racing to meet you ...

The crowds were indeed racing towards Clarence House and the red roses were quickly followed by a flood of bouquets and children's posies. At the Tower and Hyde Park there was a salute of guns. RAF planes wrote the letter E in the sky. Parliament sent its congratulations, an unprecedented honour for a Queen Consort on her birthday.

For the evening's climax Queen Elizabeth had chosen the Royal Ballet at Covent Garden and the opening night of her friend Sir Frederick Ashton's *Rhapsody*. Rhapsody it was, from the first moment when with her enchantingly youthful smiles she entered the opera house surrounded by her family, through the star performance, to the grand finale when a shower of silver petals descended from the ornate ceiling. After the ballet, she met the entire company and staff on the stage, to share with them her magnificent birthday cake and admire the balloons. Some of these were heart-shaped and their messages floated above her head: 'Happy Birthday', 'We Love You'; or just 'Queen Mum'. Nothing more was really needed for in those two words everything had been said.

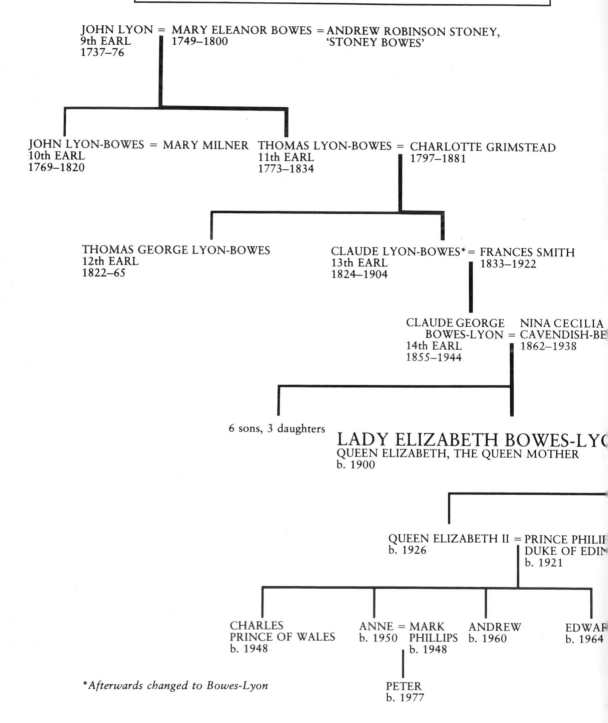

EARLS OF STRATHMORE AND KINGHORNE

JOHN LYON = MARY ELEANOR BOWES = ANDREW ROBINSON STONEY,
9th EARL   1749–1800   'STONEY BOWES'
1737–76

JOHN LYON-BOWES = MARY MILNER   THOMAS LYON-BOWES = CHARLOTTE GRIMSTEAD
10th EARL   11th EARL   1797–1881
1769–1820   1773–1834

THOMAS GEORGE LYON-BOWES   CLAUDE LYON-BOWES* = FRANCES SMITH
12th EARL   13th EARL   1833–1922
1822–65   1824–1904

CLAUDE GEORGE   NINA CECILIA
BOWES-LYON = CAVENDISH-BE
14th EARL   1862–1938
1855–1944

6 sons, 3 daughters

LADY ELIZABETH BOWES-LYC
QUEEN ELIZABETH, THE QUEEN MOTHER
b. 1900

QUEEN ELIZABETH II = PRINCE PHILII
b. 1926   DUKE OF EDIN
                     b. 1921

CHARLES   ANNE = MARK   ANDREW   EDWAF
PRINCE OF WALES   b. 1950   PHILLIPS   b. 1960   b. 1964
b. 1948   b. 1948

*Afterwards changed to Bowes-Lyon

PETER
b. 1977

Family Tree of Queen Elizabeth
The Queen Mother

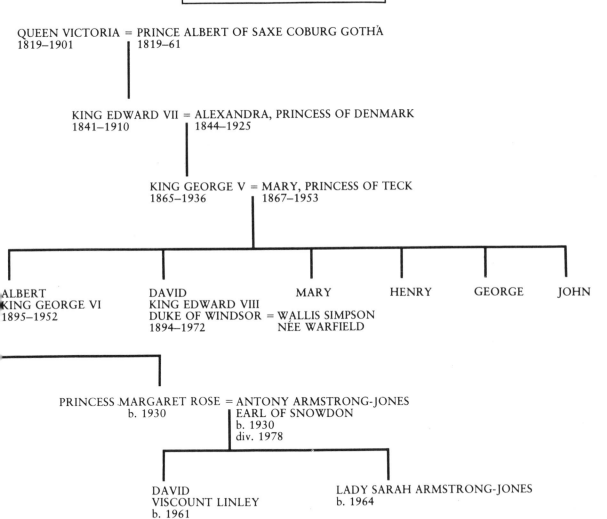

THE ROYAL FAMILY

QUEEN VICTORIA = PRINCE ALBERT OF SAXE COBURG GOTHA
1819–1901   1819–61

KING EDWARD VII = ALEXANDRA, PRINCESS OF DENMARK
1841–1910   1844–1925

KING GEORGE V = MARY, PRINCESS OF TECK
1865–1936   1867–1953

ALBERT
KING GEORGE VI
1895–1952

DAVID
KING EDWARD VIII
DUKE OF WINDSOR = WALLIS SIMPSON
1894–1972   NÉE WARFIELD

MARY   HENRY   GEORGE   JOHN

PRINCESS MARGARET ROSE = ANTONY ARMSTRONG-JONES
b. 1930   EARL OF SNOWDON
b. 1930
div. 1978

DAVID
VISCOUNT LINLEY
b. 1961

LADY SARAH ARMSTRONG-JONES
b. 1964

Acknowledgments

The publishers have taken all possible care to trace and acknowledge the ownership of illustrations. If we have made an incorrect attribution we apologize and will be happy to correct the entry in any reprint. ·

Photographs and illustrations are supplied or are reproduced by kind permission of the following:

The pictures on the copyright page and pages *19, 26, 41* are reproduced by gracious permission of H.M. the Queen (Royal Archives, Windsor)
The pictures on pages 6, 24, 56, 62 (above) are reproduced by gracious permission of H.M. Queen Elizabeth The Queen Mother
Courtesy of Gilbert Adams: *39* (Bertram Park)
Associated Press: *106, 143*
BBC Hulton Picture Library; *title page*, 9 (below right), *19 (below), 26, 31 (below), 32, 38, 52, 81, 82*
British Tourist Authority: *123*
Camera Press: Front and back jacket (Norman Parkinson), front endpapers (right) (Norman Parkinson), frontispiece (Norman Parkinson), *contents page* (Cecil Beaton), *83*, 110 (Baron), *113* (Baron), *114* (Cecil Beaton), *115, 118, 134* (Cecil Beaton), *138* (Norman Parkinson), *144* (Norman Parkinson), *153, 161* (Snowdon), *175* (Norman Parkinson), *176–7* (Norman Parkinson), *178* (Cecil Beaton), *179* (Norman Parkinson)
Central Press: *20, 34* (above and below), *35* (below), *72, 84, 116* (below)
Mary Dunkin: *27, 37, 63* (below), *86*
Fox Photos: *45, 75, 76, 77, 85, 88, 90, 94, 96, 100, 101, 104, 112* (above), *127* (below), *133, 156* (above), *164–5*
Tim Graham: *146, 150* (above), *166, 168, 169* (above)
Guildhall Art Gallery: *42–3*
Hamlyn Group, Country Life Books: *11, 13, 40, 80, 159*
Eileen Hose: *66, 129* (Cecil Beaton)
Anwar Hussein: Front endpapers (left), back endpapers (both), *137, 150* (below), *155, 156* (below), *163* (below), *171, 172, 176* (above and below)
Illustrated London News: *Half-title page, 54, 55, 92*
Imperial War Museum; *91*
Keystone Press Agency: *53, 74, 120*
Mansell Collection: *14* (E. O. Hoppé), *19* (above right), *22*
J. MacDonald: *157*

National Portrait Gallery: 9 (below left)
Popperfoto: *46, 47, 48, 52, 62* (below), *63* (above), *69, 70, 79, 87, 105* (above), *116* (above), *124, 127* (above), *139*
Press Association: *28, 107, 136*
Private Collection: *93*
Sport and General: *149, 151* (above)
Syndication International: 9 (above left and right), *13* (below left and right), *17, 23, 33, 44, 50, 112* (below), *132, 151* (below), *177* (below)
Times Newspapers: *73, 108*
Weidenfeld and Nicolson Archives: *31* (above), *33, 35* (above), *57, 98, 105, 163* (above)

Designed by Martin Richards
Picture research by Mary Dunkin
Index by Vicki Robinson
Numbers in italic type refer to black and white illustrations

Index